Praise for *Ready, ~~~, ~~~~*

"Loads of wisdom is packed into these pages! The in-depth examples Curtis and Bener offer touch upon a variety of leader personalities, cultures, and geographies in North America, with obvious application on other continents. I will be using this book with the church planters I coach and teach for years to come! It is a must-read in the field of new church development."

—Paul Nixon, President of The Epicenter Group,
Author of *Cultural Competency* and *Launching a New Worship Community*

"Finally, an honest, smart, and accessible look into the business of church planting! Packed full of useful stories, insights, and models, this theologically grounded work will help with the Who, What, Where, When, Why, and How of starting a new faith community. This nuts-and-bolts book will give any aspiring church planter the knowledge and tools needed to hit the ground running. I highly recommend it."

—Rev. Jerry Herships, Founding Pastor of AfterHours Denver,
Author of *Last Call* and *Rogue Saints*

"Practical, authentic, engaging, entertaining, and educational. A must-have for every ministry toolbox. If you're wondering how to get started as a church planter and need a step-by-step guide, this is the most practical and Spirit-inspired book you will find."

—Rev. Dr. Frank Beard, Bishop,
Illinois Great Rivers Conference of The United Methodist Church

"Whether you have heard God's call to plant a new church or you are a leader overseeing the planting strategy of your conference, *Ready, Set, Plant: The Why and How of Starting New Churches* is the best place to start and the perfect resource to share with planters. This book offers a practical guide to planting and inspiring stories from the combined experience and wisdom of the authors. Together, Bener and Curtis guide readers to the right questions for each step of the planting process and building a solid foundation in sustainable church planting."

—Junius B. Dotson, General Secretary & CEO of Discipleship Ministries,
Author of *Soul Reset*

Dear Dave,
I know you love reading books.
So, here is another one. Enjoy your
reading. And, thank you for encouraging
to write and publish my own book.
Blessings,
Kuya
Bener
26/01/2021

READY, SET, PLANT

The **WHY** *and* **HOW**
of Starting New Churches

Bener Agtarap and Curtis Brown

DISCIPLESHIP
RESOURCES
NASHVILLE

Front cover images: Shutterstock.com
Cover design: Marc Whitaker
Interior design: PerfecType, Nashville, TN

Print ISBN: 978-0-88177-946-2
Mobi ISBN: 978-0-88177-947-9
Epub ISBN: 978-0-88177-948-6

From Bener

Extremely grateful to my wife, Clarita, and my children, Sola Kristie, Katriel Kairos, and especially Kiyah Karmia, whose support and encouragement helped me in writing this book

From Curtis

With thanks to my co-laborer in the harvest fields, Meredith

CONTENTS

ACKNOWLEDGMENTS

Both of us want to acknowledge the collaborative and cooperative community of leaders of the global new church planting movement within The United Methodist Church. We are especially grateful for the passion, knowledge, and dedication of those who have been a part of The United Methodist Path 1 movement for starting new churches. Several sections of this book have been shared through workshops, handouts, and presentations as part of Path 1's work, including the models of new faith communities in chapter 8, the process of gathering the first twelve people to a new ministry in chapter 10, and the description of the heart of a planter in chapter 12. The collective work of our colleagues, workshop participants, and new faith community planters has repeatedly improved our thinking in these sections. Special mention should be given to Paul Nixon, Sam Rodriguez, Candace Lewis, Kim Griffith, and William Chaney for their contributions, edits, and corrections.

The discussion of planting strategies in chapter 6 was first introduced as part of Curtis's unpublished research dissertation at Garrett-Evangelical Theological Seminary, *Relational Church Planting: A Study of Newly Started United Methodist Churches Utilizing the Relational Principles and Practices of Community Organizing*.

Doug Ruffle, director of Community Engagement and Church Planting Resources for Discipleship Ministries of The United Methodist Church, has walked with us through every step of envisioning, writing, and producing this book. It would not be here without his able assistance and guidance.

We are especially grateful for the new faith community planters who allowed us to interview them, hear their stories, and retell them to you:

Mitch Marcello, Rachel Gilmore, Jasper Peters, Rodrigo Cruz, and Aaron Saenz. We are inspired each day by what God is doing through the lives and ministries of the planters we have been honored to know. It is a privilege to serve Christ alongside each of them.

1

Introduction to Planting

> Jesus went about all the cities and villages, teaching in their synagogues, and proclaiming the good news of the kingdom, and curing every disease and every sickness. When he saw the crowds, he had compassion for them, because they were harassed and helpless, like sheep without a shepherd. Then he said to his disciples, "The harvest is plentiful, but the laborers are few; therefore ask the Lord of the harvest to send out laborers into his harvest."
>
> —MATTHEW 9:35-38

As a disciple of Jesus, your purpose in life is to fulfill the mission of God that all human beings and all of creation should be filled with the love of God. This love is a gift from God (see John 3:16). God's love is shown in Jesus: "[God] sent his one and only Son into the world that we might live through him" (1 John 4:9, NIV). If your desire is to follow Jesus, your mission is to do the will of the One who sent him (see John 6:38). Your mission is far greater than your denomination's missional mandate or even that of your wildest aspirations and dreams: Your primary mission is God's mission.

Before his departure, Jesus left his disciples with a commission to "go and make disciples" (Matt. 28:19, NIV). He departed with an assurance that his disciples would take responsibility for the continuation of the good work of sharing the love of God with all God's children in the world. Jesus believed in this bunch of disciples as believers who would lead in this effort of disciple making as a strategy for advancing the gospel, an effort that is grounded in the love of God and powered by the Spirit of the risen Christ, which is living and life-giving.

Like you, every disciple of Jesus is a "missioner," an active participant in *missio dei*—"the mission of God" or "the sending of God." Today, more than two billion of Christ's disciples can be found across the globe and in every corner of the earth. They are known by their love through their work of mercy and justice. They participate in the life and ministry of faith communities or churches that embody the life-changing gospel of Jesus Christ. These disciples are living out their call as leaders and partners of God in celebrating the reign of God on earth.

As agents of change, many examples of personal regeneration and social transformation are happening as a consequence of their actions. A great example is from the Urban Poiema Church in Milwaukee, Wisconsin, which has allowed us to share Larissa's faith story of coming from a background of abuse, addiction, and brokenness to being led by God to the loving community of Urban Poiema, which changed her life and helped her find her own calling. After encountering the awesome love of God through the warm embrace of fellowship and care from the other followers of Christ in this new church, Larissa is now serving the church as the evangelism director and leading the church's efforts in connecting more people to Jesus' love. She is one of the many examples of people who have become disciples of Jesus now actively participating and leading in the mission of making disciples and changing the world in Jesus' name.

Near the end of his life, John Wesley wrote,

> I am not afraid that the people called Methodists should ever cease to exist either in Europe or America. But I am afraid lest they should only exist as a dead sect, having

>the form of religion without power. And this undoubt-
>edly will be the case unless they hold fast both the doc-
>trine, spirit, and discipline with which they first set out.[1]

Even more today, we need to make our Christian witness alive, vital, and great as it continues to participate in the mission of God. In the United States of America, early Methodists received John Wesley's words and applied them earnestly. As people began migrating west in mid-1776 in great numbers and at a fast rate, the people called Methodists used this reality as an opportunity to plant new churches. As people moved, so did the church planting. As new people swept through the land, new churches formed as well. The strategy of going where the people were going worked out very well in early Methodism in the United States. We haven't seen this kind of a movement of church planting in the United States since then, but that doesn't mean that it can't happen again in our lifetime. This phenomenal achievement has happened before; it is our turn to make it happen again. We need to believe and behave again as a *movement*.

One thing we can glean from the Methodist experience is that the vitality and greatness of our Christian witness largely depends upon our commitment to fulfill the mission of making disciples of Jesus Christ. The church journeys with new disciples as they continue to grow in faith and as they become agents of God's transformative work in the world. We should not lose our focus on our mission: *disciple making, transforming the world*. We should embrace the shifting and diversifying mission field as a monumental moment to make a difference in the lives of many people and in many places in the world in the name of Jesus. Thus, our efforts of making new disciples by forming new faith communities can help us fulfill our contribution to God's mission.

The good news is that the movement Jesus led more than 2,000 years ago is still making a huge difference in many people's lives, as well as in many communities and nations throughout the world, even to this very day. That is why we are in the mission of forming new disciples of Jesus Christ, so that the work of changing lives and transforming communities will never cease. As we focus our efforts on making new disciples, those new disciples will then form new churches. We make disciples who will plant new churches that will transform the world! It takes disciple-making and church-planting efforts to sustain this transformative movement of the gospel. Our vision for a movement that serves both the present and future generations is the paramount reason for our existence as a church.

Our Changing World

We find ourselves in exciting times in which we have both the opportunity and the capability of reaching, connecting to, and engaging with multitudes of people through a variety of new and fresh expressions of a community of faith. According to Rev. Michael Baughman, the founder of Union Coffee church in Dallas, Texas, and editor of the book *Flipping Church: How Successful Church Planters Are Turning Conventional Wisdom Upside-Down,*

> Although Jesus is at the heart of what we do at Union Coffee . . . we did not plant our church to bring God to the neighborhood or Jesus into the lives of those who walk in our doors. We believe that God is already at work in our neighborhood, that Jesus is already at work in the lives of the people who walk in our doors. Our responsibility is to see what God is doing in our neighborhood and become a part of that.[2]

This new expression of church clearly points us to the primary motive of church planting. The goal of starting new churches is so that more people can take part in God's transforming mission in the world.

Among church planters, there is wide agreement that the United States is becoming one of the largest mission fields in the world. We know the following realities are happening in the United States and that they will continue to develop into the future, and we need to take them into account as we carry out God's mission moving forward in this country.

1. We are witnessing the increasing immigration of people into this country practically from all countries in the world. According to data from the US Census Bureau released in 2019, "The United States has more immigrants than any other country in the world. Today, more than 40 million people living in the U.S.

were born in another country, accounting for about one-fifth of the world's migrants. The population of immigrants is also very diverse, with just about every country in the world represented among U.S. immigrants."[3] The steady and uninterrupted flow of new people coming to this country naturally expands diversity in population in terms of age, ethnicity, and culture such that it makes this country an important mission field. Unfortunately, many churches don't know what to do with the changes happening within their neighborhood, while others are seemingly not interested in dealing with this new reality. Consequently, a significant number of these local churches are declining in membership and losing connection with the growing number of new people coming into their neighborhoods.

2. We are seeing a rising number of people disaffiliating themselves from organized religion, even while many young adults are showing interest in spirituality and Christianity. It is fascinating to imagine on one hand that there is a steady decline or closure of established Christian churches or institutions, while on the other hand, there is this consistent quest among the younger generations of today for finding meaning, purpose in life, and God. How can the Christian community, especially local churches, be equipped to engage the people in their community with the gospel of Jesus Christ?

3. We are noticing the growing number of groundbreaking, innovative, and entrepreneurial forms and expressions of new churches and new faith communities that are springing up each year across the country. These novel approaches in starting new churches are becoming more popular and have been found to be effective in building connections between church people and non-church people. As we continue to see the rise of these strategies, the key question we will wrestle with is not so much one of church-planting models or strategies but rather the question of leadership. What leadership skills, gifts, and talents are needed to effectively carry out innovative and pioneering approaches to church planting? Where do we find them? How can these leaders get excited about joining the disciple-making and church-planting movement in the United States?

Given the continuing social, economic, political, and even religious divide among people and communities in the United States and in the world, Jesus' prayer still needs to be prayed and acted upon by Christians and other people of faith who may choose to embrace its message: "Thy will be done in earth, as it is in heaven" (Matt. 6:10, KJV). Many people are looking for meaning or purpose in life; many are searching for hope and courage to move on in their daily living; many communities are working for justice and peace for the sake of their children in the neighborhoods. Junius B. Dotson, chief executive officer and general secretary of the General Board of Discipleship of The United Methodist Church, has said, "People aren't products, profits, or goals. They aren't simply the means to an end; they represent the total focus in what we do. People are the means. People are the end. People are the middle in all that we do. Successful institutions understand that people are not 'the how,' as in *how* we reach our goals, but they are 'the why' of our involvement in the first place."[4] As you read, we hope that you will accept the call and will step forward to be the channel of hope for people through the gospel of Christ.

We are happy that you picked up this book. It tells us that you care about reaching new disciples by starting new ministries, new faith communities, new congregations, and new churches. Whether you are doing church planting as a lead planter or part of a church-planting team; as part of the leadership of a church-planting network and denomination; as a layperson or group of laypeople in a local church dreaming of starting a new ministry or faith community; or as someone who is still in the process of discernment about church planting, this book is for you. Why? Simply because we believe that it takes a diverse group of people who work together to fulfill the mission of spreading the love of God to all nations and transforming the lives of all God's people. We hope that as you read this book, it will strengthen your resolve to be part of the adventure of starting new churches, faith communities, and ministries. And we hope that the process outlined in this book will help you better see and appreciate your gifts and graces as a leader for church planting.

What's in This Book?

At the heart of this book is our understanding that new churches and new faith communities emerge from the unique gifts, strengths, and talents of planting leaders. As you will see, the content follows this structure:

- **Introduction to Planting** (chapter 1) sets the biblical and missiological foundation of church planting based on the life and works of Jesus and his early followers as recorded in the Bible and how it impacts our participation in the gospel work in today's world.

- **Why Plant?** (chapter 2) explores these three foundational inquiries: (1) Why Jesus? (Christology); (2) Why New Disciples? (missiology); and (3) Why New Places or Churches? (ecclesiology).

- **Why Leads to Who** (chapter 3) asserts that the reasons we have for starting a new ministry determine whom we envision as a leader of that ministry or whether we envision ourselves as potential leaders. For example, if our "why" is to make disciples, then we will look for disciple-making leaders, whether they are clergy or lay. We'll also look at how a specific church planter navigated this transition in a new church. This chapter will tell the planter story of Mitch Marcello and The Acts Network.

- **Who Is a Planter?** (chapter 4) describes who can start new things and how to identify their potential in terms of their gifts, strengths, experiences, behaviors, and characteristics as leaders. This chapter also includes specific questions and processes for individual and collective discernment of calling and giftedness in starting a new ministry.

- **Who Leads to How** (chapter 5) stresses that the gifts and strengths of the planter (the "who") determine the strategies and approaches best used for starting a new faith community (the "how"). More relationship-focused leaders might begin with meeting a lot of new people. More autonomous leaders might set out on their own, while more collaborative leaders will begin with partnerships and team building. This chapter highlights the planter story of Rachel Gilmore at The Gathering.

- **How Are Churches Planted?** (chapter 6) discusses the current methodologies and key strategies for church planting and how to use the best assessment tools for better understanding and application of approaches to starting new things.

🌱 **How Leads to What** (chapter 7) points out that the strategies used to gather and inspire a group of people into discipleship will shape the model of new ministry. Whether it is a "parachute drop," multisite, church within a church, fresh expression, spiritual entrepreneurship, or restart, the model of organization emerges from the strategies and practices used by the planting leader or leaders. To illustrate this transition, we will meet Jasper Peters and the Belong Church in Denver, Colorado.

🌱 **What Is a New Faith Community?** (chapter 8) answers questions such as, "What is a new faith community?" "What new ministries are there that might not be described as new faith communities?" "What kinds of resources are needed for different strategies and models of church planting?"

🌱 **What Leads to Where** (chapter 9) emphasizes that the gifts of the planter, the strategies of building Christian community, and the organizing model all inform the location or target audience for any new ministry. This often includes an analysis of available resources, such as partner churches, supportive permission-giving from other established church leaders or denominations, prayer networks, financial support, facilities, and other materials. This chapter features the planting story of Rodrigo Cruz and The Nett Church.

🌱 **Where to Plant?** (chapter 10) focuses on these two questions: (1) "Where should we start a new church?" and (2) "Where can we find the necessary resources?" This includes how to analyze demographics and evaluate potential partners and facilities for new ministries.

🌱 **Where Leads to When** (chapter 11) affirms that with a firm strategy and with a clear sense of the Holy Spirit's guidance, almost any time is the right time to take a risk on inviting new people into new ministries that help them transform into new disciples of Jesus Christ. In this chapter, we will talk with Aaron Saenz about starting the multisite Valley Praise United Methodist Church.

♡ **When Do We Start?** (chapter 12) will dwell on the question, "When is the right time to start something new?" We will examine the importance of strategic evaluation, adjustment, and innovation and how best to use them along the journey. And we will also invite you to join us in this adventurous life within the arena of making new disciples of Jesus in new places, new ministries, new faith communities, and new churches.

There is no solitary approach to new-church development, and no one will tell you that it is an easy enterprise; it is not. In fact, there are many ways to start a new church, and many interconnected factors come into consideration in different stages of starting a new church or faith community. Simply put, it's a complex undertaking. While there are lots of books, trainings, and studies done in church planting that can give you directions for what you should do and for what a new church should look like, it is your call to discern and determine where to begin your journey.

Our Hope

We hope that this book will give you a strong and solid starting point for the adventure ahead. And it starts with you as the church planter. We believe that effectively developing new faith communities or new churches starts with the gifts and capacities of the church planter. Based on our research, study, and long-term experience in church planting, we believe that other factors such as location, demographics, planting models, and resources are not the starting point for planting a new church, a new congregation, a new faith community, or a new ministry. It is you—the leader. However, each one of these factors has to be carefully and strategically considered by church planters and their church-planting team if they wish for their church plant to stay strong and bear fruit—much fruit.

We are often asked about the chances for saving a denomination mired in conflict. While we believe that new churches can help us keep our sights set on the big picture, we must respond that saving a denomination is not the primary motivation; spreading scriptural holiness across the land *is* a primary motivation. We plant new churches and mobilize our congregations for mission work because the world needs a new generation of Christ followers forming their families, churches, communities, and our society in ways that honor the truly good news of the gospel of Jesus Christ in all ways.

And we start with ourselves, by making a shift from being a disciple to becoming a disciple maker. That is a commitment to the mission of making and sending disciples to engage people in the community with the gospel of Jesus Christ. In turn, they become active participants in making more disciples as agents of transformation in the world, following the way of Jesus through the inspiration of the Spirit of God.

In Jesus' perspective, it is good that we believe in Christ and that we do the works of Christ. However, Jesus expects more from every person who believes in him. Jesus said, "They will do even greater things than these" (John 14:12, NIV). Indeed, we can do greater things for the glory of God. Let us do the works of Jesus and do "even greater things" with God's love in Christ Jesus.

> Therefore God also highly exalted him
>> and gave him the name
>> that is above every name,
> so that at the name of Jesus
>> every knee should bend,
>> in heaven and on earth and under the earth,
> and every tongue should confess
>> that Jesus Christ is Lord,
>> to the glory of God the Father. (Phil. 2:9-11)

This is about you because Jesus is in you!

2

Why Plant?

"Very truly, I tell you, the one who believes in me will also do the works that I do and, in fact, will do greater works than these, because I am going to the Father. I will do whatever you ask in my name, so that the Father may be glorified in the Son. If in my name you ask me for anything, I will do it."

—JOHN 14:12-14

For many years, we've talked to countless numbers of church planters about these questions: "Why start new churches? Why have you decided to devote your life to starting a new church?" We have also studied church-planting movements in many countries and have discussed these questions with the leaders of the various church organizations across the globe. All of them—each and every one—pointed to their own experience of God's love that stimulated their desire to share that love with others by forming new churches or faith communities.

If we are to make disciples of Jesus Christ in the United States and elsewhere in the world, we need to begin with a clear understanding and a strong grasp of the width and depth of God's love in our own lives. Thus, our church-planting efforts, if they are really about helping people connect with the love of God in Jesus' name, should be a reflection of the beloved community of God. Therefore, our "why" for church planting should be formed, normed, and sustained by these two great commandments: "'You shall love the Lord your God with all your heart, and with all your soul, and with all your mind.' This is the greatest and first commandment. And a second is like it: 'You shall love your neighbor as yourself'" (Matt. 22:37-39). The true church of Christ is known by our love. Jesus says, "By this everyone will know that you are my disciples, if you have love for one another" (John 13:35). Thus, any community that fails to reflect this mark of love is not a church, because the purpose of the church's mission—the "why" of its being a church—is to invite people to be in loving relationship with God and with one another, grounded in Christ Jesus.

We can encounter this love of God in and through Christ Jesus. As the scripture says, "The Word became flesh and lived among us, and we have seen his glory, the glory as of a father's only son, full of grace and truth" (John 1:14). We develop new faith communities in Jesus' name so more people will get a chance to experience the fullness and unfailing love of God through Jesus. We plant new churches so that many will see the glory of God's children at work in the world. As a church planter, your responsibility is to lead people to knowing Christ and to walk with them as a fellow follower of Christ. You invite new disciples to grow in their faith and service along with other disciples of Jesus as together, you share the love of God with all God's children in need of God's welcoming and redeeming love.

Who Is Jesus?

We need church planters with clarity of their call to lead others to Jesus. Leading others to Jesus, however, can be done effectively only if one knows who Jesus is. At the heart of the matter is Jesus' question to his disciples in Matthew 16: "Who do people say that the Son of Man is?" And the disciples responded, "Some say John the Baptist, but others Elijah, and still others Jeremiah or one of the prophets" (vv. 13-14). Jesus probably was not really interested to know what people said about him. He more likely wanted to know what his own friends said about who he was. Jesus still wants to know our answer to this question as modern disciples of Christ in this present day. Jesus replied to the disciples, "But who do you say that I am?" (Matt. 16:15). If you don't know who Jesus is, you probably shouldn't be in the business of building a church of Jesus. "Simon Peter answered, 'You are the Messiah, the Son of the living God.' And Jesus answered him, 'Blessed are you, Simon son of Jonah! For flesh and blood has not revealed this to you, but my Father in heaven. And I tell you, you are Peter, and on this rock I will build my church'" (Matt. 16:16-18).

Rev. Douglas Ruffle, author and director of Community Engagement and Church Planting Resources of Path 1 at Discipleship Ministries of The United Methodist Church, gives a beautiful description of Jesus' life in a "Study Guide on Why Jesus?" in Path 1's Lay Planter Training. He writes:

> [Jesus] lived an extraordinary life to the fullest more than 2,000 years ago. Born into a poor family under the poorest of circumstances, his mother gave birth to him in a place among animals—a stable or cave—in a little town of Palestine. His parents fled his birthplace, living as refugees in a foreign land for fear of death from the ruling leader. They returned to another small town, which was despised by many. He learned the craft of carpentry and observed the religious life of a Jew. As an adult, around thirty years of age, he began to teach and preach in the towns and countryside.
>
> He was called "rabbi" by followers. He invited hearers to receive God's coming governance of the world and to live by the principles and values of that realm. The followers who gathered around him and learned at his feet were ordinary people who had worked ordinary jobs. He healed the sick; he ate with people who were ridiculed and despised by members of society. He broke barriers of race, culture, and religion to be fully present to and relate to men and women, some of whom were considered "sinners" by others from the community. He brought life out of death for a young girl and raised an older man from the dead. He despised the desecration

of God's holy temple by those who would turn it into a sales bazaar. When entering the most important city of the region where he lived, he was celebrated as the one who had been promised of God. One of his closest followers, a man named Simon Peter, confessed to him that indeed, he was the Messiah, the long-awaited redeemer of Israel.

And yet, Simon Peter and his other followers abandoned him when he was arrested and tried by the rulers in the city. His followers hid, while he was whipped and a crown of thorns pushed on his head. He was forced to carry a heavy, wooden cross through the city; he was spat upon and ridiculed and then hung on the cross he had carried; spikes pierced through his hands and feet, and he was placed between two common criminals. Three days after he died on the cross, some women followers said that he was raised from the dead and continued to live and appear among those who had been closest to him. This Aramaic-speaking Jew never published writings; yet, because of the testimony of those who knew him—*their* writings, *their* teaching, *their* preaching—this one became the most influential person in western history and—some would say—the world. Art, music, literature, and architecture extol him. Many followers died for him. They affirmed, with the psalmist, that "Your constant love is better than life itself" (Psalm 63:3). Today his followers count in the billions.[1]

Why Jesus?

One of the greatest followers of Christ was John Wesley, founder of the Methodist movement. He had a transformative experience at Aldersgate Street in London on May 24, 1738. John Wesley's life-changing encounter with God led to the development of one of the most influential Christian movements in the history of the world. Wesley writes:

> In the evening, I went very unwillingly to a society in
> Aldersgate Street, one was reading Luther's Preface to
> the Epistle to the Romans. About a quarter before nine,
> while he was describing the change which God works
> in the heart through faith in Christ, I felt my heart
> strangely warmed. I felt I did trust in Christ, Christ
> alone, for salvation; and an assurance was given me that
> He had taken away my sins, even mine, and saved me
> from the law of sin and death.[2]

Many claim that John Wesley's life-changing encounter with the love of God has been the bedrock and heart of Methodism.

Millions of people have been touched by the love of God through the mission and ministry of the people called Methodists since the beginning of the Methodist movement in Great Britain some 280 years ago, its historic growth in the United States in the 1800s, and its ongoing witness in the present day and age in many nations across the globe. Today, the mission of The United Methodist Church is to make disciples of Jesus Christ for the transformation of the world. Church planting is a ministry focus area of the whole denomination. According to a denominational report on their church-planting activities through the Path One New Church Starts movement,

> Path One has a list of new faith communities reported
> by each annual conference for approximately the past
> two quadrennia, 2008–2016. . . . It turned out that when
> duplicates are eliminated between lists for the two qua-
> drennia, there are 1,059 new faith communities reported
> to Path One during these years. . . . Many new people
> have been reached. From this sample, over 43,000
> people worshiped in the past year in one of the new
> places established. From this data, one can infer that the
> total from all the starts during the past two quadrennia
> reached almost 100,000 worshipers.[3]

All these new faith community worshipers have their own story to tell about how their lives and communities have been transformed by the love of God—a story that each of these people represents as a living witness to the gospel story of Jesus and as a powerful inspiration for our efforts to start new churches.

The Jesus story has shaped civilizations and culture for more than 2,000 years. We know that Jesus is like us; and so, in him, we can find our humanity. Jesus shows us how to live fully for God and for others. As a leader, Jesus sets an example by his words and deeds full of grace and rooted in God's love. As his followers, we must ask ourselves, what compelling reason might there be to follow Jesus today? Why Jesus?

Mahatma Gandhi was a big admirer of Jesus. He showed his admiration and respect for the life and teachings of Jesus. Unfortunately, Gandhi did not seem to experience this love and the teachings of Jesus with the Christians in India in his time. He was purported to have said, "I like your Christ, I do not like your Christians. Your Christians are so unlike your Christ." Supposedly, he added, "If Christians would really live according to the teachings of Christ, as found in the Bible, all of India would be Christian today." This is a sad commentary on Christians.

Bener's Story

Not every person has experienced Christians in a similar way as did Gandhi. Bener shares a powerful story of the church's influence in his life. He writes:

> I had a much more positive experience with Christians. I was eleven years old when I encountered Jesus through the community outreach program of young Methodists in our hometown. I was born into a devout Roman Catholic working-class home in Navotas, a lowly fishing town just north of Manila. I learned to live simply and shared meager resources with my family. My parents, Benito and Erlinda, were labor union leaders. Raising their four children was not easy, but they did it very well. My parents taught us the importance of fairness and justice. They also raised us in faith and devotion to God. Most Filipinos born and raised in the rural agricultural fields and poverty-stricken urban centers of the Philippines shared in this bond of blood, sweat, and

tears because they loved their families and wanted the best of what they could afford to live an abundant life.

In the midst of the political and economic turmoil of the late 1960s–early 1970s, I was growing up with little appreciation for myself. I remember my insecurity, self-doubting, and uncertainty about my future. It was during this time of self-defeat when I encountered God in my life. Through the vacation Bible school extension ministry of Saint Peter United Methodist Church, located in our neighborhood, the youth volunteers of this extension ministry helped all the kids understand that every person is a beloved child of God. As a child who knew the harshness of poverty and isolation, the church's outreach through this program was a warm embrace that comforted my young soul. My love affair with God had begun, and my encounter with God's love became, and still is today, the cornerstone of both my being as a child of God as well as my doing as a disciple of Jesus Christ. I'm here to testify that the main and only reason why I have devoted myself to and immersed myself in the task of church planting is so that others could share in the blessings of faith in God and love of God that I received as a child.

Why Plant New Things?

John Wesley's encounter with the love of God was not exclusive to him, nor was it an isolated experience for us and for others. Many people have encountered God in the past, and many people still encounter God today. Here is the compelling reason why we are actively pursuing the task of creating new places, new communities of faith, and new churches: We connect with God's children, regardless of age, gender, and nationality, to offer the love of God in their lives. We take them with us on our journey of faith so that all of us can find our place to participate in the mission of making disciples of Jesus Christ for the transformation of the world. God is still calling people to God's amazing love, even more so today. As church planters, we take our task with great joy and honor in joining God to plant and grow God's love in the hearts of all the people in the world.

As church planters, our goal is to invite as many people as we can reach to see and to join our churches or faith communities. Whenever we see our people sharing the love of God with one another, we rejoice because the presence of God is in our midst and in the hearts of everyone. The church becomes a visible sign of God's reign. As we grow in love of God and with one another, we have the confidence to go where the people are; we take courage in offering Christ's love in an authentic way. We welcome them to grow with us as disciples of Jesus and to get involved in the mission of God.

People will know who we are by our love. Every church should be known by the way its members care for one another and for the whole creation. Some churches are known for their worship, preaching, and music; others are known for their great youth and children's ministries; while still others are known by their great location, beautiful building, and spacious parking lot. These characteristics are useful if your objective is to get the attention of people to come and visit your church. However, if your church's goal is to keep people growing in faith and continuing their participation in the life and ministry of your congregation, it is important that your whole effort is driven by love—your love of God and love of others. The early church in the New Testament lived out this love very well. As a result, the members received "the goodwill of all the people. And day by day the Lord added to their number those who were being saved" (Acts 2:47). Indeed, the early followers of Jesus as a community of faith were the embodiment of the life and teachings of Jesus that are rooted in love.

If our mission is to multiply disciples of Jesus by planting new churches, it is clear to us that we need to develop churches like the church in Acts 2:

> They devoted themselves to the apostles' teaching and to fellowship, to the breaking of bread and to prayer. Everyone was filled with awe at the many wonders and signs performed by the apostles. All the believers were together and had everything in common. They sold property and possessions to give to anyone who had need. Every day they continued to meet together

in the temple courts. They broke bread in their homes
and ate together with glad and sincere hearts, praising
God and enjoying the favor of all the people. And the
Lord added to their number daily those who were being
saved. (vv. 42-47, NIV)

We are convinced that this is the kind of church many people today would
love to be part of—a kind of church that mirrors Christ!

We agree with the commentary made by Jim Griffith and Bill Easum
in their book *Ten Most Common Mistakes Made by New Church Starts*:

> The Great Commission minus the Great Commandment
> reduces evangelism to a vocation, a challenge, or a duty.
> However, the deep motivator for people who take evange-
> lism seriously is an overwhelming love of God. The Great
> Commission is the inevitable outflow of a heart filled
> with a love for God. The impetus for planting a church
> has to be a desire for people to experience this love, not
> simply to carry out some mandate from the past.[4]

This means our task of starting new churches should be done in loyalty
to Christ and to his mission of fulfilling the message that says, "In Christ
God was reconciling the world to himself, not counting their trespasses
against them, and entrusting the message of reconciliation to us" (2 Cor.
5:19). Ushering people into a reconciling relationship with God, with one
another, and with the whole creation is the most important thing the
church can do for the world.

The world needs the gospel of Jesus. The gospel has the power to
change not only the human heart but also the world itself. Taking the
gospel seriously will help us to be clear about one thing: It is God, not
us, who changes the lives of people and transforms the world. As church
planters, we must plant, water, and cultivate the gospel in the hearts of
women and men, children and adults, rich and poor. But if our efforts of
planting a new church do not reflect this message of reconciliation and
forgiveness, it is merely a human enterprise and therefore a misrepresen-
tation of the God of the harvest who invites all people to be embraced by
God's love. If God's love is true, it is true for everyone; this is the theology of church planting. It really is as simple as that. The task of a church

planter is simply to live this simple truth about the love of God and to invite others to experience God's love and grace. Churches that subscribe to this simple truth are the ones whose members will bear fruit, for they bear the name of Jesus.

Bener's Church Planting Mission

Bener continues his story:

> I remain thankful for the opportunity to serve God as a church planter. I am indebted to those who introduced me to Jesus, to Christ's church, and to his mission. My journey in church planting began thirty-six years ago, when I started a new faith community in Kaunlaran Village. It was in this place that I encountered Christ in a deeper way. Like Moses, who met God at the burning bush; Paul, who encountered the risen Christ on the road to Damascus; and John Wesley, who encountered Christ at Aldersgate, I encountered Christ in Kaunlaran Village.
>
> Kaunlaran Village was originally a fishpond located on the north side of the City of Manila. Due to a growing problem of lack of housing for poor urban families who live in Manila and other neighboring cities and towns, the Philippine government converted this vast land into a low-cost housing project for urban poor. Several thousand families moved into this new community to make a new beginning. But starting a new life in a new community proved not to be that easy or smooth. The lack of basic services such as electricity, drinking water, and sewage, as well as the unavailability of jobs and other sources of income, made it even more difficult to adjust in this new housing settlement. On top of all this were social problems such as illegal drugs; gambling; theft; and crime, including extrajudicial killings or the "salvaging" of presumed criminals. All of these contributed to the hardships of people who now found themselves permanently living in this new village.

It was during this time of transition when I got a
call to plant a new church in such a place as this. As
a church planter, I knew from the get-go that this new
church should be active and effective in both evangelistic and social outreach. This new church should make
the most difference for the gospel in the personal, social,
economic, and spiritual lives of the people in this new
community. During our first public worship, I preached
on John 3:16. And I admonished those present to believe
that this new church that we were launching in this
community in the name of Jesus would be a visible sign
and presence of the amazing love of God. Thus, we
would be a local church that is a mission outpost of the
gospel.

We have to ask ourselves these questions: What are our compelling
reasons for investing our lives in the task of starting new churches or faith
communities? Is it the biblical mandate? Is it because the world needs
the gospel? Is it a desire to pass along our faith, beliefs, and tradition as
Christians from our generation to the next generation? Are we starting
new churches grounded in Christ? Is the good news of God's love in Jesus
the bedrock of these new churches?

Remember, the reasons you have for starting a new church determine
whom you will envision as a church planter of that new faith community.
We will explore this topic more in the next chapter.

3

Why Leads to Who

I will not venture to speak of anything except what
Christ has accomplished through me to win obedience
from the Gentiles, by word and deed, by the power of
signs and wonders, by the power of the Spirit of God,
so that from Jerusalem and as far around as Illyricum
I have fully proclaimed the good news of Christ. Thus
I make it my ambition to proclaim the good news, not
where Christ has already been named, so that I do not
build on someone else's foundation.

—ROMANS 15:18-20

The reasons we have for starting a new ministry determine whom we
envision as a church planter of that new faith community. For example, if
our "why" is to make disciples, then we'll look for disciple-making leaders,
whether they are lay or clergy. If our "why" is to create organizations to
support a denomination financially, we'll look only for denominationally
loyal clergy. Motivations matter and can broaden our understanding of
who can lead or how they can form a church—or they can restrict the
horizon of possibilities until it only includes creating a church that looks
just like the churches we already know.

We learn this principle from the example of the apostle Paul, who we believe to be the most prominent leader of the Christian movement after Jesus. Paul's aim is none other than "to proclaim the good news" (Rom. 15:20). In his letter to the followers of Christ in Rome, he writes, "Thus I make it my ambition to proclaim the good news, not where Christ has already been named, so that I do not build on someone else's foundation" (15:20.) It was this ambition of Paul's that led him to reach out beyond his Jewish roots to the Gentiles to proclaim the good news of Jesus Christ. Paul's missionary movement spread from Jerusalem across the Roman world, and it reached people who did not know Christ's name in those places. All the things that Paul accomplished throughout his life in ministry demonstrated his missional purpose. His reason for ministry made him one of the greatest missionary leaders in the history of Christianity, one whom many of us seek to emulate.

In a church-planting movement, we hope to identify, equip, and deploy leaders, both clergy and lay, who clearly understand their "why" or purpose. Their reason for participating as leaders in making new disciples of Jesus Christ by forming new churches or faith communities is what matters most in this field of ministry.

Planter Story: Mitch Marcello and the Acts Network

Mitch Marcello is the leader of the Acts Network at First Church, a United Methodist congregation in Williamsport, Pennsylvania. Mitch is a layperson. He doesn't call himself a church planter, nor does he want that designation. Instead, he sees himself as someone whose role is to empower laity to go out and create faith communities. His ambition is to equip, deploy, and engage in ministry with laypeople to create fresh expressions of a community of faith. He is not a church planter but an equipper and coworker of lay leaders. Mitch's clear understanding of his purpose guides his approach and practice in helping this network of multiple new faith communities to grow while keeping its relationship with First Church.

The Acts Network currently consists of a group of thirteen expressions of new faith communities that are part of the larger community at

First Church, with all of them working together as one unit in seeking
methods for engaging the people in their community in creative, innovative, and organic ways. In describing the relationship between the First
Church and these thirteen new faith communities, Mitch explains,

> All of these are part of the same church. It's just a lot of
> different communities that make up the same faith com-
> munity. Think about New York City. It is composed of
> a bunch of diverse, beautiful communities that all make
> up the Big Apple. Increasingly, we want to see a church
> with a bunch of diverse faith communities but [where]
> all are part of one church family.

Prior to the creation of the Acts Network, Mitch was on staff at First
Church, working in college and campus ministries. At the urging of
the pastors, the staff began exploring different ways of being a church
together. They started pondering the question, What would it look like for
us to engage a different population of people? Mitch says that they began
asking this question because they were

> becoming more aware of what was happening cultur-
> ally—how the culture was shifting [in a way] that results
> in fewer and fewer people coming to church on a Sunday
> morning. Essentially, what we were learning and seeing
> firsthand was that what we were doing and what we have
> been doing for a very long time simply wasn't connect-
> ing or isn't connecting with the people it previously was
> connecting with.

The leaders at First Church found themselves clueless for a time about
how to respond to this essential question in an adequate way. They simply didn't have an idea about what to do next to try to effectively connect
with the new people whom they knew and encountered each day in their
mission field.

But God sent help. Mitch recalls:

> There was a student in the seminary who contacted us
> to ask if he could do a paper or a project in coordination
> with a church that actually might do something with his

work. And so we said, "Sure, why not? No skin off our
back, right?" His name is Kris Sledge, and he came up
with this thing [that would come to be] called the Acts
Network. . . . Instead of wanting to reach out and form
a single community with a thousand people, [he asked,]
how about creating a hundred communities with at
least ten people in each community? What would that
look like?

These adaptive questions raised by this student inspired Mitch and other
leaders at First Church to begin to imagine this picture of a network of
one hundred new faith communities, with at least ten people participating in each group. The excitement kicked in. More questions were raised,
and one of these questions was, "What do we do?" The church leaders
determined that the plan they would need to execute this vision had to
conform with their reason for starting this new thing—that is, a network
that equips laypeople to engage other laypeople in the community in a
variety of fresh expressions of what it means to be a faith community in
Jesus' name.

So, Mitch and the other leaders at First Church started to think differently, which led them to the point where they put together a ministry
proposal for the launching of the Acts Network. They shared their vision
and sought the assistance of their denominational conference of churches
to partner with and support this initiative through a financial grant for
pursuing this work. In turn, the conference leaders also realized that they
needed to do their work differently because what they had been doing had
not been working. They were in search of a new approach to new church
development in the region and thought that this new network might be it.

Subsequently, following more research, strategic conversations, and
experimentation, the lead pastor of First Church asked Mitch to meet
with him in his office. Mitch recalls Pastor Matt Lake saying to him, "Hey,
I think you're the guy to [lead] this. Would you be willing to apply [for the
job]?" Mitch was offered the position, and the Acts Network began to take
shape. Initially, it appeared that little was happening. Mitch says,

From the start, I knew that my goal was not necessarily
for me to go out and start all of these things myself. But
it was to find people who had bright eyes, find people

who had passion . . . and then empower them to go and do that work. And so, again, the first six months, because I wasn't out there specifically doing that myself, we didn't have any groups going. People looked at me like I was crazy.

At this point, Mitch realized that if he wanted to see this initiative work, he needed to be clear about his purpose in doing this ministry. And for Mitch, knowing the "why" of being a leader in this work has been the key factor in its success. With a new clarity of purpose, Mitch and his teammates began to see the vision coming together. Mitch proudly describes some of the earliest activities:

The very first thing was a nature hike where . . . they would do devotions . . . pray at different spots. They would do Communion once they reached the top. . . . So, they were able to connect with other hikers and other people who connected to nature.

Fit Faith was formed and lasted for about two-and-a-half years, and that met in a local gym. So, there was a personal trainer, [and] we got to invite people into that moment and have a time where our active worship was lifting [weights] together. . . . And that's where we had our first baptism from the Acts Network. Here's how it happened: Somebody was coming there who hadn't walked into a church in fourteen years. We were playing tennis one day, and we were talking about one of our devotionals, and . . . we talked about baptism and what it meant. . . . [This person's] curiosity and interest in Christianity grew as he continued to show up and hang out with our group. He took his faith journey seriously, and so, he was baptized in front of a congregation on Christmas morning that same year. That was a beautiful moment for us.

There's one [ministry] that started simply as a neighborhood game night—and that's still going to this day. . . . We began to look at our homes as more of a mission field, and that's what we began to do—invite our neighbors, invite people who [were] no longer connected in different ways into a moment where we got to build community. And for about the first year, that's all we did. As time has gone on, it's grown into a place where we've done worship, and we've prayed and laid hands on each other and shared the highs and lows. When you think of church, the church has happened.

We also have dinner-church at a place called The Pajama Factory on Monday evenings. . . . Now, that's specifically [geared] toward building a community meal, but we invite people to Thursday evenings for Bible studies. We're exploring worship this spring. So, we've been building this community. We have talent shows and other fun activities. This has been going on for a little over a year now.

The Acts Network is a living and growing organism. This network will continue to grow and make an impact in the lives of many and in communities where they may find themselves doing gospel work. The strategy is simple yet very effective: Go and engage people where they are. As a result, Mitch says, the network has developed into all kinds of emerging groups, "from a rugby church to a swing-dancing church to house worship to dinner-church to pub theology to something called *shinrin-Yoku*—which is essentially nature church—to college worship in coffee shops." Some of these communities look more like established churches, while others do not, and they continue to grow into new forms and ministries as the participants explore discipleship. And in the meantime, the followers see the church taking shape in the midst of that.

The Acts Network lives out an incarnational ministry that attracts about 150 regular participants and about 300 to 325 people in their orbits of extended-relationship networks. Every time they come together, they enjoy the freshness of what it means to be disciples of Christ within the network of multiple fresh expressions of the community of faith in Jesus' name. And sharing the blessings of the gospel and being part of a community are the primary motivations for people's active participation in this fellowship.

The tremendous success of the Acts Network and how it is thriving are attributable to the reason why it was started: to unleash God's people into the world to journey with others in a loving relationship with God through Christ Jesus by forming new faith communities.

There are several key learnings we can take from the Acts Network. First, for people to know Jesus, we need to step out in bold ways. And in many ways, we need to shed parts of the old structures that have been too rigid, because they have hindered us from actually seeing where we can go, being incarnational in places that are outside the church, and connecting with people who are disenfranchised or unwilling to walk into a conventional church building. In the process of engaging people to know Christ, these church people experience growth in their knowledge of Christ in their lives. As God's people share this life with Christ with their friends and neighbors, their faith becomes alive as they are accompanied along the way by other disciples of Jesus—a life-changing experience. Strengthening relationships with fellow members of the group and growing together as a community in their discipleship journey is the primary goal of this initiative.

Second, every disciple of Christ can be part of this faith adventure. Mitch explains:

> We define *play* as a curiosity-driven exploration. As we step out in these different ways, we get to discover and encounter God in ways that either we haven't before or haven't in a very long time. . . . And so that's a huge theological underpinning for the Acts Network, the theology of play.

Everyone can be part of it and experience the joy of sharing faith and love of God with others who also seek to belong in a beloved community of God. In this community, every person is welcomed, affirmed, and involved in building a relationship with fellow disciples of Jesus Christ.

Mitch continues:

> This grand adventure isn't reserved just for staff or missionaries or pastors or the super-holy. This is actually a calling and an invitation for every single person who has given their life to Christ.

The Acts Network is the type of initiative that can help us all find our way back to the right lane of making disciples of Jesus Christ by releasing our laypeople to connect with people in their neighborhoods.

Third, there is a focus on lay leadership. The Acts Network is intentional about equipping its laity, who are called and respond to the call to be in this ministry. Mitch meets with his fellow network leaders for monthly check-ins, and they have hired a couple of coaches who also meet with the group leaders every month. Coaching is an integral part of their leadership development and support program. There are also quarterly moments when the entire Acts Network group comes together for joint training, fellowship, and mutual support. They continue their efforts to invite other laypeople to get involved in growing this initiative, either as leaders or as part of a group. And they continue to see some people stepping forward and exploring those possibilities for themselves.

Fourth, the Acts Network is not a program. According to Mitch,

> This is about engaging ministry in a different way. And if you're walking into this thinking that you're going to get a cookie cutter or receive everything that you need and just apply it, you're going to be disappointed and perhaps discouraged. But if you're willing to truly be incarnational and listen and love people where they are, God just moves in the midst of that.

It is a process of finding, equipping, and deploying laity to engage their friends, neighbors, and loved ones by coming together as a community of people who want to experience God in a fresh way.

The apostle Paul in the New Testament and Mitch Marcello of the Acts Network are just two among many examples of people who responded to the call to start new communities of people who seek to grow in their relationship with God and with one another and to make a difference in the world. These leadership examples demonstrate that the reasons we have for starting a new ministry determine whom we envision as a church planter of that new faith community.

In church planting, we need to find those leaders who clearly understand their reasons for stepping into this adventure of creating new ministries or new faith communities. But although that is a critical step to take under consideration in new church starts, there are other questions that are just as crucial in this work, questions such as: Who can start new things? How do we identify these leaders? What are the steps we need to take to help them discern their call to church planting? What are the gifts and characteristics of church planters? We will explore these and other questions in the next chapter.

4

Who Is a Planter?

You are a chosen race, a royal priesthood, a holy nation, God's own people, in order that you may proclaim the mighty acts of him who called you out of darkness into his marvelous light.

> Once you were not a people,
>> but now you are God's people;
> once you had not received mercy,
>> but now you have received mercy.
>
> —I PETER 2:9-10

Leadership matters, and after discerning a call from God, leadership is the most important ingredient in starting a new church, ministry, or faith community. Leaders have planted growing, life-changing new ministries with little money in regions of decreasing population and with almost no encouragement. More than financial resources, more than available meeting spaces, more than ministry partners, more than training, more than population growth, leadership is the most critical ingredient. Good leaders find ways to thrive and make the most of difficult situations, while poor leaders find ways to flounder, no matter the opportunity. If leadership is so critical in planting new ministries, what makes for good planting leaders, and where can they be found?

Historically speaking, starting new ministries has been primarily a lay endeavor with clergy support. We see this in the New Testament-planting stories, with lay men and women taking the lead in gathering and forming new congregations. We see this in the history of the Methodists in the United States, where lay preachers planted a new congregation seemingly in every village, train depot, or wide spot in the road. Today, we can see the exponential growth of lay-led planting movements in the rapid growth of churches in places such as the Philippines and China. Clergy are in support and leadership-development roles, but laypeople are the primary community builders and evangelists. This is in keeping with the foundational Protestant doctrine of "the priesthood of all believers." It is clear that the Holy Spirit dispenses gifts of discipling and organizing upon the entire church, clergy and laity alike, and these gifts are the key to forming new faith communities. The only ordination required for church planting is that which is granted at baptism into the priesthood of all believers.

This is not to diminish the role of clergy. Lay planters need the support, the training, the encouragement, the prayers, and the investment of clergy leaders. Clergy have specific callings to word, sacrament, service, and order in the church, but not all of these are exclusive privileges of the clergy. Indeed, in starting a new church or ministry, people skills are much more important than professional education or denominational credentialing. This is especially true during times of great societal change, when deep innovation is needed. Enthusiastic amateurs have been at the heart of almost every movement of disruptive innovation. Well-trained professionals are excellent at managing incremental change and gradual improvement within an organization or profession; but deep, radical, foundational change almost always arises from those outside the organization or profession. These new leaders bring a new approach with new practices that find new ways to envision or execute the organization's mission. Given the tectonic changes occurring in the spiritual lives of people and the community-building practices happening across the globe, the mission of Christ is in desperate need of precisely these kinds of spiritual entrepreneurs who can launch innovative forms of Christian community.

Lay church planters bring an additional benefit in that they can be quickly trained, which allows for a more rapid multiplication of leaders and ministries. Because of their need to perform well across the broad portfolio of required tasks for ministry generalists, it takes professional clergy a long time to develop, train, and become credentialed. In addition to training in such traditional skills as preaching, theology, sacraments, biblical scholarship, pastoral psychology, and spiritual formation, today's clergy also need to learn skills in a wide variety of disciplines such as organizational development, fundraising, community organizing, marketing, media production, and nonprofit management. Becoming competent in such a wide range of skills requires a great deal of time invested in professional training and gathering experience. This makes credentialing and multiplying new clergy leaders an expensive endeavor for any church, and it can cripple a rapidly growing movement of the Holy Spirit. The church either finds itself asking new believers to wait for a clergyperson or it finds itself deploying partially trained clergy who may not be up to the task. Lay planters, however, are specialists who do not need to be trained as ministry generalists. Serving in partnership with other ministry specialists or well-trained clergy generalists, lay planters can focus on the essential tasks of sharing the gospel, discipling new believers, and gathering people into a new faith community.

An overreliance on clergy to start new congregations also tends to result in new faith communities looking a lot like established churches that are led by resident clergy pastors. Clergy tend to emphasize the skills and practices that they found successful as pastors within the congregations where they were trained. Subsequently, they tend to plant new churches that need them to be good at those same skills and practices.

But our traditional view of a "church" is not the only kind of faith community that can thrive in today's societal environment, and we will need more than traditional "pastors" to serve these faith communities. If we are going to see a diverse expression of forms of Christian faith communities, we will need to deploy a wide variety of diversely trained new faith-community planters. Chaplains are needed for the faith communities that are emerging in partnership with other work, education, health care, and artistic communities. Bivocational planters are needed for faith communities that are emerging in the workforce, business, and marketplace. Guides and rangers are needed for faith communities that are emerging within outdoor recreation and pilgrimage journeys. Elders and sages are needed for faith communities that are emerging within immigrant, ethnic, and cultural minority groups. Activists are needed for faith communities that are emerging out of social and political advocacy groups. Teachers are needed for faith communities that are emerging alongside schools, universities, and educators. Entrepreneurs are needed for faith communities that serve as incubators of personal, corporate, and societal innovation.

The Holy Spirit does not honor the boundary between sacred and secular workplaces, and the church is being reborn through emerging Christian faith communities across our society. These new forms will need new leaders.

Where to Find Planting Leaders?

The greatest barrier for churches in starting new ministries or new faith communities is the perceived lack of available and capable leaders. This leadership deficit has led some large churches and judicatories to abandon church-multiplication strategies even though they can see the need for new ministries, have the financial resources for launching new ministries, and understand that God is urging them to reach new people through new ministries. Too often, however, this perceived lack of leaders arises from a lack of a comprehensive leadership-development process and a failure to understand the behaviors and competencies that lead to the successful planting of multiplying ministries.

The first step to finding planting leaders is to cultivate an organizational culture of taking risks with new ideas and innovations in ministry. For potential planters who are already involved in the established church or organization, a culture of risk-taking gives them the opportunity to grow from taking smaller risky steps of faithfulness to taking larger and riskier leaps. A culture of risk-taking will also tend to attract and retain people who have a higher risk tolerance and who might be more inclined to begin innovative or entrepreneurial ministries. Cultivating a risk-taking culture begins with leaders modeling and promoting appropriate risk-taking for the sake of the mission. When leaders risk their power, reputation, and person in following Christ, then others will join them. A risk-taking culture emphasizes trust and support for risk-taking leaders, especially when they lead new ventures that partially or completely fail. Regularly celebrating the leaders of both successful and failed innovations is the single most important habit in building a risk-taking culture. All innovation is seen as an experiential opportunity to try new things, to see how they work, and to learn together the ways God is leading into the future.

The second step in finding planting leaders is to build deep partnerships with other disciple-making organizations and faith communities. If the mission is to multiply disciples of Jesus Christ, then a new ministry will need leaders who already know and understand how to multiply disciples. Within all the streams of Christianity, the vast majority of established churches are more focused on caring for the people who are already part of their church than they are focused on making disciples of the people who do not yet go to a church. However, within every part of the church there are groups, congregations, movements, and organizations that are consistently and effectively helping new people to initiate a journey of knowing and following Christ. These places can become incubators and greenhouses for new leaders who fully understand and participate in discipleship multiplication. Some historic centers of disciple making have included camp and retreat centers, youth and campus ministries, spiritual-formation and revival ministries, newer congregations, and evangelistic outreach ministries. Often, people who are relatively new to following Jesus can make excellent evangelists themselves, as they are less likely to have isolated themselves within a cocoon of church thinking. With appropriate organization and supervision, it is quite possible to help new believers become planters of new ministries. Disciple-making organizations and ministries can also be excellent training grounds for potential planting leaders. By nesting new ministry leaders as interns or residents into one of these organizations, they can learn the practices and organizational culture that makes for effective discipleship multiplication.

The third step in finding planting leaders is to invest in growing leaders through an intentional system of leadership development. Most accomplished leaders are not found; they are grown. Effective churches and organizations assist potential leaders by offering mentoring, coaching, training, apprenticeships, inspiration, and learning opportunities. A leadership development system grows out of answering these questions:

   ♀ What kind of leader is needed for the church's mission?
   ♀ What are the behaviors of an effective leader for that mission?
   ♀ What experiences help develop those behaviors?
   ♀ How long does it take to become that kind of leader with those behaviors?
   ♀ What determines when someone is ready to be that kind of leader?

Once these principles are defined, they will determine the necessary experiences and learning opportunities. The most effective leadership-development systems are less focused on classroom trainings and more focused on individual mentoring relationships. All leadership-development systems will require investment of organizational resources and leadership to consistently perform over a long period of time. This investment, however, is one that will repay dividends of new generations of new leaders innovating new ways to reach new disciples of Jesus Christ.

What Are the Leadership Characteristics of Planters?

Leadership characteristics grow out of a person's natural gifts and talents, which are then honed through practice into strengths and behaviors. Behavior is the outward expression of leadership characteristics and the most important result of good leadership. When looking for new leaders, pay closer attention to witnessed behaviors than to expressed preferences or opinions. Past behaviors are the best indicators of future behaviors. This means that recruitment and identification of potential leaders requires observation in more than just an interview. In seeking potential planting leaders for new ministries, churches, or faith communities, look for five behaviors that frequently appear in emerging planters.

1. **Restlessness because of the gospel.** Potential planters are generally unsettled with "business as usual" and seem to overflow with ideas, hopes, plans, and visions of what the church could become if it would more fully live into the gospel.
2. **Habitual pushing of boundaries.** Potential planters present a challenge to existing organizational structures and authorities.

Depending on their personality, this can be interpreted as problematic or arrogant behavior by their ministry supervisors or mentors.

3. **Impatience with institutional culture.** Potential planters see an urgency about their ministries. They frequently operate at a faster pace of initiation and innovation than the comfortable pace of their church or organizational culture.

4. **Constantly trying new things.** Potential planters have a high risk tolerance, and they will try many different ideas and approaches to find one that works for their mission, context, and resources. Even with relatively successful actions, they will often continue to try new improvements or may even seem to grow bored with last year's idea in order to start something new.

5. **Gathering people to causes or activities.** Potential planters have a track record of gathering people together. In both big and small groups, they forge relationships, inspire collective action, and nurture groups into cohesive and connected relationship networks.

These behaviors are not a final list of strengths, skills, or characteristics of a potential planter, but they are commonly exhibited by successful planters. These behaviors indicate a person who could probably be assessed and possibly be equipped to start a new ministry, a new congregation, or a new faith community.

There is no one simple and universal set of skills needed to plant something new. Given the wide variety of ministry contexts, the multiple expressions of forms of ministry, the wide differences in available resources and partnerships, and the bewildering array of gifts and blessings provided by the Holy Spirit, it should be no surprise that successful planters themselves are extremely varied. God has created the world's diversity on purpose, and diverse planters are a gift to a diverse world. Successful planters understand their uniqueness and use their gifts and skills in ways that match their ministry context, partners, resources, and mission. Some key aspects of self-understanding for potential planters include the following:

1. **Spiritual giftedness.** The Holy Spirit provides a wide variety of gifts for building up the body of Christ. These gifts are meant to

be used, and all gifts from God are helpful. Planters are not just apostles or evangelists—many also have the gift of assistance as they help new disciples discover Christ for themselves or as they assist a group of new disciples in organizing themselves into a new ministry or faith community.

2. **Group affinities.** All planters have a unique life experience that has equipped them to connect more easily with some people than with others. This is called *affinity*. Affinity can be built around many different factors, such as life stage, work experience, cultural or ethnic background, generational identity, immigration experience, education, political affiliation, hobbies, or neighborhood. Affinity comes in two parts—from those with whom the planter finds it easier to build relationships and from those who find it easier to build a relationship with the planter. These are not always the same groups. Affinity is important to understand because it is easier to gather people within an affinity group. However, affinity is also important to understand because it can expose undiscovered bias within the planter that might put artificial limits on the planter's evangelistic imagination. God has in mind to include all kinds of people, and planters need to understand how their own preferences might be keeping them from seeing a call to reach beyond the societal barriers of racism and classism to discover a deeper affinity with unexpected people.

3. **Leadership style and strengths.** Effective leaders come in a variety of styles with different strengths, but they all understand their style and adopt practices to fit their style to the leadership needs of their team and situation. Some leaders are encouragers, constantly connecting with and cheering on their teams. Some leaders are strategists, with a thousand ideas and contingency plans to help their team achieve its goals. Some leaders are caretakers, making sure all the members of their team have all that they need to fully express their own strengths. Some leaders are drivers, always casting a compelling vision of a changed tomorrow that propels their team into action. There is no single preferred leadership style for a successful planter, and God has used all of these styles to help launch new ministries. Instead, successful planters all share a commitment to use their leadership style and

strengths in service of Christ's mission and a willingness to grow into new ways of leading that bring out the best in their teams. This is often expressed in their capacity to receive and grow through effective coaching.

4. **Personality style.** Given the intense focus on meeting and gathering with a lot of people, extroverts are often seen as having a natural advantage as planters. This is especially true in the early stages of starting a new ministry, when the focus is entirely on developing relationships. Extroverts tend to build new ministries more quickly, but they also have more difficulty delegating relational tasks to other leaders. Subsequently, the ministries they plant tend to stall out when there are too many people involved for the extroverted planter to relate to personally. Introverts take more time to build the initial group, but they are more able to multiply other leaders and create systems for a new ministry to grow beyond a single relationship cell. Planters who understand their own personality style are more likely to build a complementary and diverse team of leaders that can more effectively pursue their shared mission.

5. **Cross-culture communication style.** People are, in no small part, a product of their culture. Culture conditions a host of expectations and assumptions about how people should interact. Successful planters understand their own cultural assumptions and know how to navigate the cultural expectations of the people they are gathering. Culture can determine things such as how comfortable people are with direct confrontations, how familiar strangers can be upon first meeting, how motivated a person is by the group's collective goals that might not be his or her own specific individual goals, and how much deference might be afforded an elder or a person in a position of leadership. These cultural mores are often thought to be barriers between ethnic groups, but culture is broader than just ethnicity. Regardless of ethnicity, people from rural communities may tend to operate with a sense of time that is not necessarily connected to a clock. It is time to begin a gathering not when the clock displays the starting time but, instead, when everyone has arrived and is settled. Planters can discover their own preferences through self-reflection, and

they can discover the cultural patterns of others through careful research. Some people are already more competent in communicating and relating across cultural differences, but all can improve their capacity for this.

What Are the Key Behaviors of Planters?

Even with the wide variety of characteristics of successful planters, almost all of them display five common behaviors that they are already practicing in their lives. These may show up in their personal life, in their profession or occupation, in their hobbies, within their family, or in current ministry leadership roles. These behaviors are usually so integrated into their lives that they may not have thought much about them. Significantly, these are current behaviors and not things that they hope to do in the future. Again, past behavior is the best predictor of future behavior. These behaviors are critical to a planter's well-being, success, and spiritual life, and the lack of one of these behaviors should raise deep questions about that person's readiness to plant a new ministry or faith community.

The first behavior is that **a planter sees the world through the eyes of Christ**. This means that the planter's focus is on offering the compassionate love and grace of Jesus Christ to people. A planter views other people not as potential "butts in seats" to grow the church but as beloved children of God whose lives will be enriched by a relationship with God through Jesus Christ. Planters see the world around them in non-transactional terms, caring less for what they can receive from others and more about what they can offer. This vision also opens planters to deep heartbreak for their neighbors, community, and world.

The second behavior is that **a planter has a deep, joyful, and persevering faith in Jesus**. Planting a new ministry will bring profound moments of discouragement, several late nights filled with worry, and repeatedly tempting opportunities for abandoning or diluting the difficulty of the new ministry. Planting is a full-contact sport, in which planters are up close and personal with the people they are gathering. There is very little distance possible between the planter's personal and pastoral identity, so planters need to give careful consideration to the depth of the integration of their personal life, their faith, and their calling to plant something new. At its most basic level, the only thing that a planter has to offer is the witness to God's love that is evident in his or her own life. New people will want to examine the planter's faith to see if Christian discipleship is worthy of their own commitment. Planters who have journeyed through difficulty and remain filled with the joy of their faith have a powerful witness. As they move through the difficulty of planting a new ministry, they will need to rely on this enduring faith.

The third behavior is that **a planter already knows and loves people who don't like church**. Churchgoing Christians, especially clergy, live in insular relationship bubbles where they spend almost all their time with other people who already go to church. Starting new ministries that make new disciples requires spending a lot of time with people who do not like church and who have chosen not to participate in readily available expressions of Christian community. In previous generations, new church planting relied upon gathering new people by attracting churchgoing Christians who were new residents or who were looking for a new church because they were dissatisfied with their previous church. This strategy was reasonably effective in building new churches when a large portion of the local population was already Christian. However, focusing on transfer growth is less effective in many places around the world, and it often results in churches that have few adults who are making first-time professions of faith in Jesus Christ. In short, if you want to help people become disciples of Jesus Christ, you have to love spending time with people who aren't Christian.

The fourth behavior is that **a planter has a demonstrated history of starting new things**. People who thrive on starting new ministries, churches, and faith communities will have begun gathering and organizing people into new projects, groups, clubs, events, businesses, committees, and ministries from a young age. They might recall organizing their neighborhood friends into a lawn-mowing business, helping launch a scouting group, writing and producing an elementary-school play, starting a student website, organizing a petition drive, or rallying people to change a societal problem. Planters will display their drive and capacity to lead new things by having already done so. This drive, of course, can be supported and nurtured by an effective system of leadership development, but planters often display this drive even in the face of opposition and resistance. If planters are still exploring their capacity to lead new initiatives, they can be given a few lower-risk opportunities to continue to grow in skill and confidence. It's important to note that not all these new projects need to have succeeded. Planters grow and learn through failure as well as success.

The fifth behavior is that **a planter has a demonstrated history of multiplying disciples**. For potential planters who are clergy or are already leaders in established churches, this is the most critically necessary behavior. The process of multiplying disciples includes two practices—helping new people begin to follow Jesus and coaching followers of Jesus to help other new people begin to follow Jesus. This multigenerational discipling is the key to exponential growth. Planters will be able to recall multiple experiences of both practices. When asked, they will often be able to recount several encounters within the last week when they were able to enter into a spiritual conversation with people and invite them to take the next step of faith. This can be in their church setting, such as during a class or individual meeting; but often it is in their personal life, as they describe conversations with their neighbors, friends, or strangers. Planters will also be able to talk about someone they've helped to become a disciple of Christ who is now helping others to enter into a journey of discipleship. Potential planters can learn these habits of disciple making by immersion experiences in organizations, churches, movements, and groups that have discipleship multiplication as a core part of their culture. If potential planters are not enculturated into discipleship multiplication, they may do an excellent job of helping to grow a new ministry or church filled with good "church folks," but they will struggle with planting a new movement of disciple-making, world-changing followers of Christ.

How Are Planters Discerned?

For those who feel the yearning to start a new ministry, congregation, or faith community, their first task is discerning a call from God to plant and assessing their capacity to answer that call. This involves the personal exploration of their sense of calling and the collective affirmation of potential partners, mentors, and supporters. Books about starting new things love to recount the myth of the "heroic entrepreneur" whose individual vision drives him or her to overcome all obstacles without any help from others. The more commonplace reality, however, is that the most effective planters have a large network of supporters who provide assistance, advice, finances, resources, introductions, encouragement, and intercession. For this reason, discernment needs to be both personal and collective.

Personal discernment involves planters seeking answers to a series of questions that they ask themselves. Do they see in themselves the gifts, behaviors, and characteristics of a planter? Do they have a sense of calling from God to plant a new ministry, new church, or new faith community? Do their close friends, family, and household members affirm their gifts and calling to plant something new? Do they have sufficient knowledge and understanding of the risks, costs, and difficulties of planting to make an informed decision? Do they see themselves filled with joy doing the hard work of planting something new? Have they earnestly, prayerfully, and thoughtfully done the work to determine that this is a calling from God? Answering these questions can take time, and it can involve multiple conversations, retreats, research, training experiences, and explorations of new ministries.

Collective discernment involves the external assessment of a planter by potential partners, supporters, mentors, and investors. By necessity, collective discernment is less subjective and relies on more objective measures. A key facet of collective discernment is the ability of the potential planter to share his or her confidence, calling, and competencies with a group of informed potential supporters. This is not dissimilar to the work of sharing a vision for a new ministry with potential participants.

However, the personal charisma of a potential planter should not be the only criterion for assessing a calling to plant. The most effective tools for assessing a potential planter are behavior-based interviews and onsite observations. Behavior-based interviews have been used for decades in organizational hiring and evaluation. During the interview, candidates are asked to talk about a time when they displayed a behavior that is a necessary part of the position they are considering. A typical behavior-based question begins with, "Share a story of a time when you . . ." This is different than asking planters about their beliefs or motivations and instead focuses on their practice of the behaviors of planters. Of course, questions about what planters believe about doctrine, morality, and professional boundaries are appropriate, but they are significantly less revealing than asking planters about times when they have translated their beliefs into actions in specific situations.

Personal and collective discernment is often aided by a well-developed and well-defined formal process of planter assessment. This process of assessing potential planters involves helping planters learn about themselves, learn about their mission field, and learn about their capacity to answer a call from God to plant in that mission field. These results are shared together with a well-informed and spiritually mature group of potential supporters. Together, they engage in conversation, prayer, and mutual learning about the planter's capacity. The process usually involves a series of self-discovery methods designed to clarify a planter's strengths, leadership style, personality type, conflict style, and cross-cultural competency. There are multiple leadership inventories and assessments available to assist the planter with this.

Additionally, the planter will seek a series of interviews and recommendations from people who have seen and understood the individual's ministry and work history. Sometimes, the assessment team will visit the planter's current ministry to make observations. Often, planters will be asked to envision the broad outlines of how they might begin a new ministry within the specific context of ministry they are considering. Not all planters can succeed in all contexts or with all planting models, so the whole assessment process should be considered in light of an actual emerging ministry possibility instead of a vague potential planting opportunity.

Finally, the planter and the assessment team should meet together for a behavior-based interview, conversation, and evaluation. This process usually culminates in a written report that outlines the planter's strengths, growing edges, ideal planting context and method, and recommendation or non-recommendation as a planter.

Assessment and discernment processes are critically necessary, but even the best process of personal and collective discernment will miss things. Look at the enormous amount of time, expertise, and money that is invested in evaluating potential players for professional sports leagues, and even with that investment, consider the high rate of players who do not live up to expectations and quickly leave the league. Any prediction of future performance, no matter how rigorous the evaluation process, will come with a high degree of uncertainty. That uncertainty does not make the discernment and assessment process useless, because it can often help planters and partners identify and avoid obstacles they might not have seen without the process. Discernment is always an ongoing process, so participants should remember to draw conclusions lightly and be prepared to adjust to the movement of the Holy Spirit. Discernment and assessment are always improved by people who understand the cultural context of the new ministry, and high levels of care need to be taken to ensure the elimination of racial, cultural, gender-based, or other biases within the process. For these reasons, an outside facilitator can often be helpful.

Every new ministry, congregation, or faith community begins with the dream of a small group of people who answer God's calling to start something new. The individual gifts and callings of these people who start a new ministry are the soil into which all the strategies, models, and plans for the new ministry will be planted. The "who" leads to the "how."

5

Who Leads to How

The gifts [Christ] gave were that some would be apostles, some prophets, some evangelists, some pastors and teachers, to equip the saints for the work of ministry, for building up the body of Christ, until all of us come to the unity of the faith and of the knowledge of the Son of God, to maturity, to the measure of the full stature of Christ.

—EPHESIANS 4:11-13

The gifts and strengths of the planter (the "who") determine the strategies and approaches (the "how") best used for starting a new faith community. A more autonomous leader might set out on his or her own, while a collaborative leader will begin with partnerships and team building. A more relationship-focused leader might start by meeting a lot of new people. Every planter does it differently, because every church planter is unique in terms of his or her gifts and strengths. And those gifts and strengths play a significant role in determining the best strategy a church planter should use in starting a new church or faith community. When the gifts of the leader and the strategy in birthing a new church match, it often generates a synergy that leads to greater impact than when there is a mismatch between the two.

Planter Story: Rachel Gilmore and The Gathering

We find this principle to be the case in the story of Rachel Gilmore and The Gathering. As an itinerant pastor in The United Methodist Church appointment system, Rachel received her first assignment to serve as a church planter. She got this call to ministry right out of seminary in the summer of 2009. Rachel never dreamed about nor expressed any interest in church planting. She was wary about being a church planter, and she strongly felt that her appointment as a church planter was not a good idea. Nevertheless, she came forward and said, "All right. I'll do it." She said yes, even though she had no vision for this new thing that they were asking her to birth. When asked what made her change her mind to accept this appointment, she said, "I'm a 'three' in the Enneagram [personality test]. I'm gritty. I like to make a difference." Rachel knew herself very well, especially her gifts and strengths as a leader. She was confident that things would go well using her leadership qualities and equipping others to make things happen together.

Rachel arrived in Virginia Beach in July 2009 to help start a multisite campus out of an established United Methodist congregation. She had ten young adults in this church who were supposed to help her start this new thing. Rachel recalls that the vision was like starting "a kind of a church within their church, because they wanted us to stay within their gym." From the beginning, Rachel was clear that the vision this church wanted her to lead was not going to work. She knew that she could better use her gifts and strengths to form a different kind of church, certainly not something like a worship service in a gym within and under the watch of an anchor church. In other words, the anchor church predetermined the specific strategy (a "church within a church") and type of church for this project before Rachel came into the picture as someone who would lead it. Indeed, Rachel found it hard to believe that this approach could work out well simply because the whole thing did not fit smoothly with her gifts, skills, and strengths as a leader.

But Rachel continued on and started to see a new vision for her appointment as a church planter. Within eighteen months in the "gym church," she had divided and deployed the one small group of ten young adults into four small groups with a vision to form several small groups that would multiply. A few months into shaping these small groups, each of the four small groups grew to about ten people in number. At this point, the gym church seemed to be doing pretty well: With an increased number of people now connecting with this new start, the gym church started a monthly soft or pre-launch worship gathering in September 2009. As they grew in numbers and momentum, they began a weekly worship service in February 2010. A growing number of young families with children and youth were steadily showing up for Sunday worship.

As things were happening quickly in the gym church, the anchor church began to have a different take on what was going on with their new campus. Rather than continuing with the style and relationships of the gym church, they wanted these new young families to eventually join their more traditional worship in the sanctuary, where their children and youth could participate in the established children's and youth ministry. At this point, their differences in vision became evident to both the anchor church and the gym church. After a prayerful discernment on what might be the next best thing to do, both groups decided to separate so that each could pursue what they believed God inspired them to do with their vision.

In the summer of 2010, the gym church had started the transition to find a new place where it could continue to pursue the vision of building relationships with young families with the gospel of Jesus Christ as well as the love and support of a new faith community. They moved into their new location in September 2010, where they continued to grow as a new church. On January 1, 2011, the bishop in the area officially separated the gym church from the anchor church so the two could vigorously pursue their God-given vision for their people. This decision turned out to be the right decision, because both had seen growth and vitality on two campuses. The two groups were separated by location but kept their unity and passion around the vision of making disciples of Jesus Christ for the transformation of the world.

Here are some lessons we can learn from Rachel's story, specifically in terms of how her gifts and strengths as a leader determined the type

of church and strategy or approach that would facilitate the birthing of a
new church or faith community.

1. **Know your affinity group and organize your work around
   them.** Rachel, with her small bunch of leaders, organized everything around the identified affinity group. She recalls,

   > I separated my one small group into four small groups,
   > namely: The YAMs (Young Adult Marrieds), the YUMs
   > (Young Unmarrieds), the Pregs and Babes, and the
   > Moms (preschool Moms Bible-study group). The Pregs
   > and Babes and the Moms were the ones growing the
   > most among the four small groups. Quickly, we realized
   > during our weekly gathering that we had more kids than
   > adults in worship.

   Rachel, being a mother to a six-month-old son and pregnant with
   her daughter during that first year after launching weekly worship, strategically used her life-stage situation plus her strengths
   as a leader in her organization of affinity groups to form this new
   church start.

2. **Go and meet your people where they are.** The Gathering
   came into being as a church mainly made up of young mothers
   and their children because Rachel was a young mother when
   she planted this new church. She recalls, "If I were not a young
   mother, we would not have had this kind of a church." Rachel
   knew where to go to meet her people—locations such as the
   parks, children's playgrounds, and other places where young
   mothers like her would take their children for fun. She and her
   son spent time with her peers, along with their children, in places
   where they supported one another as one big family. In the past,
   being a woman and a mother were deterrents in leading a church-
   planting project. In Rachel's case, it worked out very well for her.
   Being a woman and a mother allowed her to build relationships
   with the other women and mothers, whom she wanted to become
   part of this new church so they could participate together in
   spreading the love of God in the community.

3. **Know your context and play your gifts well in it.** Rachel grew up in a military family and found herself planting a new church in an area that had the highest concentration of military personnel anywhere in the world. One can quickly figure out that this ministry setting would work well for Rachel because of her affinity with her target group as well as with the overall context of people living in the general area. Rachel's leadership style, which is a mix of being sweet and friendly on the one hand and energetic and take-charge on the other hand, resonated with the vocation and lifestyle of the majority of people in this community. Rachel recalls one of her colleagues in the Peace Corps describing her as "the sweetest general you'd ever love." Rachel's lifetime experiences as a kid in a Navy family and as a member of the Peace Corps fit well in this context. Rachel strategically used her life experience and her leadership gifts to carry out a strategy that resonated with her target group in this mission field.

4. **Stay connected with your network of friends and allies.** Church planting is a team sport. It takes a collective effort by the whole team working as one unit to make things happen. Keeping the collectivity within a group is key to any successful working team. The signs of a healthy and robust team include recognizing each person's unique gifts and strengths and using them as part of the effort of the entire team. Rachel shares that during those moments when things got stressful in the life of the church plant, "instead of freaking out or trying to run away, I would turn to these Moms and Pregs and say, 'Okay, guys, we all need to go do this together.'" Staying connected and intentionally nurturing and strengthening these relationships were all helpful in moving this church plant forward amid stressful situations. Rachel describes her leadership as "directional and relational." Her directional approach to leadership worked well in the general context of this mission field among those with high regard for authority, and her relational characteristic as a leader resonated with her core leadership team as well as with other people in the church. Rachel reiterates that the key to the church plant's success in overcoming obstacles or getting things done was found when "we turned toward one another and our community."

5. **Recognize that prayer changes things.** After a few months passed in this appointment, Rachel still felt frustrated because she didn't think that this was a good appointment for her. She vented her deep concern in prayer to God. She recalls telling God,

> Seriously, Jesus had twelve disciples, and I got ten. And I don't think there is a need for this kind of a church. It's not like people who are completely disconnected from God are going to come and knock on the door of the church, telling me why they want to lead in starting a new church in their community.

That was Rachel's prayer.

God responded to her prayer right away in multiple ways. First, a woman who had no church family and who was going through a crisis came by to see if she could open up to a female pastor to share her concerns. Rachel was there. This woman talked and prayed with Rachel right there in the church office. Second, soon after this woman left, an email came in from a young family who had heard about this new church Rachel was leading and wondered whether they could be part of it. And third, Rachel got a text message from some teenagers who had lost one of their friends and who still felt depressed because of what had happened. Rachel remembers the text message, which read, "We're at Starbucks. We're depressed, and we just didn't know if you could come and talk to us. We don't know who to seek counsel from. We don't have a church."

That was it; that's what she needed to hear. Rachel ultimately submitted herself to lead in planting this new church. She recalls, "I put on my big-girl pants and started acting like a church planter. I had been hard-wired for this job in this kind of community and with this kind of people." From that day on, Rachel, her leadership team, and the whole church bathed this new endeavor in lots of prayer—they prayed together as one big family.

Rachel finally got it. Her decision to proceed with this appointment enlivened everyone on her leadership team to move forward with her to pursue their God-given vision. They believed that the reason why The

Gathering existed was "to help people reconnect to God, to others, to themselves, and to creation." According to Rachel,

> We found that spiritual nomads were experiencing this
> deep disconnect from one of those four areas or more,
> which became the vision that we embraced as a church.
> It also reminded us of who we were and what we're about
> and what our priorities needed to be.

Rachel and her leadership team were all excited to seize the moment for expanding their outreach to people who were seeking connection with God and wanting to participate in making a difference in their community and the world.

Now that they had a vision as a church and now that Rachel was all-in to lead this new church, everything then would run smoothly going forward, right? Wrong! The Gathering went through four major transitions within five years: They went from meeting in the gym of an anchor church to meeting in a performing arts theater to meeting in a warehouse and, finally, to merging with an existing church. Each of these transitions happened quickly. Every step required attention to detail. The whole process consumed much of Rachel's and her leadership team's time and energy. Rachel describes her leadership style: "I could be as strong of a leader as I wanted. Still, if I couldn't empower other people to find their leadership gifts, there was very little I could accomplish. I needed them to feel that they were part of a team." The people who are part of this new church know that each one of them has a purpose, that the church needs their help and support, and that every person can help The Gathering to make a difference in the world.

Rachel demonstrated her leadership approach that subscribes to the instructions by the apostle Paul to Timothy. In his letter, Paul writes, "What you have heard from me through many witnesses entrust to faithful people who will be able to teach others as well" (2 Tim. 2:2). The Gathering practices church multiplication by equipping people to multiply themselves through inviting, recruiting, and engaging new people to participate in discipleship and community-engagement initiatives of the church. Rachel says, "People come to church not to consume but to share what [they've] learned at church and [to] help shape and form others to become disciples of Jesus."

Within six years of leading this new church, Rachel took every opportunity to train and equip her leaders and the people in the congregation to exercise leadership in ways they felt called and equipped to do. According to Rachel, "Actually, four pastors came out of our church—three females and one male. The male is now a licensed local pastor, and the three women have all been to seminary and are leading United Methodist churches outside of The Gathering." Indeed, this new church is a place where people can connect with God and with a faith community and where they become disciples of Jesus Christ. More importantly, it is a community of faith that encourages each person to take upon himself or herself the responsibility of making disciples in Jesus' name.

The Gathering under Rachel's leadership went through a lot of challenging situations that put their commitment and strength as a community of faith to the test. But they managed to come out of these even more dynamic than before and more determined in pursuing their vision and mission as God intended for them. This new church didn't operate in a vacuum, nor were its participants disconnected from the people and the community they felt called to establish healthy and long-lasting relationships with, relationships that could bring about changes in people's lives and transformation in the community. This new faith community offered each person or family an experience of belonging, welcome, and hospitality and a pathway to discipleship.

Connection—with God, with one another, with oneself, and with creation—is the word that would describe the DNA of The Gathering. Everything that happens in this church is about helping people to make and nurture each of these connections. At The Gathering, no one operates in a vacuum. Every person is connected to a small group, and every small group is connected to the whole congregation and the community. This emphasis on making connections is one of the most tangible expressions of Rachel's type of leadership, which is relational and interpersonal. Rachel admits that part of her being relational is her "being open to hear stories of others . . . which could inform my vision—either push me deeper into the way I felt God was calling us or help me shift directions." The Gathering's commitment to helping their church's people make and keep these connections in essential areas of relationships (with God, with others, with oneself, and with creation) helped their efforts for sustaining a healthy and vital faith community.

In church planting, the gifts and strengths of a church planter determine the formation of a church. They also shape the strategy that could best achieve the vision of the new church. A mismatch of these two elements could be detrimental to the birth and health of a new faith community. In the case of The Gathering, Rachel used her gifts and strengths to guide the work of this new church to fulfill their God-given vision. And she empowered God's people at The Gathering to exercise their leadership gifts and strengths in making disciples of Jesus Christ for the transformation of the world.

6

How Are Churches Planted?

There are varieties of gifts, but the same Spirit; and there are varieties of services, but the same Lord; and there are varieties of activities, but it is the same God who activates all of them in everyone. To each is given the manifestation of the Spirit for the common good.

—1 CORINTHIANS 12:4-7

So, how do you start a new church, a new ministry, or a new faith community? It isn't very often that it happens as easily as renting a room and hanging up a sign that proclaims "Meet Jesus Here!" There is an enduring myth about church planters succeeding with this approach, but even though it occasionally worked for previous generations, it no longer works very well for today's church planters. Curtis was working with an older, retired pastor who had been a Methodist church planter in the high-growth suburbs of the early 1960s on the west coast of America. When this pastor had been planting, things were different than they are today. The planting pastor was called and assigned to start a new church while he was finishing up his last semester in seminary. He would graduate in May, be ordained in June, and begin at a new church in July. In the meantime, the denomination sent a team of summer interns to knock on the doors of everyone moving into the new suburb and ask them if they were Methodists. If the new residents identified as Methodists, they were invited to a meeting at a local school in August. The denomination bought a piece of property on a busy corner and a parsonage for the new pastor. A large and enthusiastic crowd came to the meeting in August, where the new pastor asked them to become charter members of the new church, and several hundred people did so that evening. They constituted the new congregation, set a time and place for the first worship service, elected officers, started a building committee, and then they adjourned. Voilà! A new church was started.

This strategy worked in that very unique time and place, but we don't often find similar successful experiences of this type today. A denominational-focused marketing approach works only among people with a high level of denominational loyalty. In the United States, we typically find this level of loyalty only among recent immigrant groups from places with a strong denominational presence, such as Presbyterians from Korea or Methodists from Samoa. A doorstop-visit campaign works only in communities with a lot of people who are at home during the day and who are willing to interrupt their work to entertain visitors. With changes in productivity demands on US households, most people are working more hours each week, working even while they are at home, and heavily scheduling their nonworking and after-work hours. A denominationally credentialed planter being immediately accepted as a capable pastoral leader requires a society that has both a high regard for clergy and a high respect for institutional authority. Both of these factors have significantly decreased in the United States, especially among middle-class, suburban dwellers.

As people and society have changed, our successful strategies of starting new churches and ministries have evolved to match our changed contexts. So, how do you determine a successful strategy?

Strategies for Planting

Every successful new start is unique and has followed its own idiosyncratic strategy that emerged out of the particularities of its context, its leaders, and its giftedness from God. This is what makes the "How I Started a Church" story genre so inspiring and also so frustrating. When planters tell their stories, they frequently testify as to their complete dependence upon God and their own strategic missteps along the way. These stories are tremendously inspiring and provide hope and encouragement for the listeners who are contemplating a calling to start something new. However, these same stories can be frustrating if you're seeking a specific checklist of strategies that can be plucked out of one context and universally applied. The principles often translate, but the specifics need to be reinterpreted or rediscovered in the specific context, with the specific people, at the specific time of each new start.

That said, you can group planting strategies into generalized categories by thinking about their first steps:

- ♔ Fellowship-first strategies
- ♔ Worship-first strategies
- ♔ Discipleship-first strategies
- ♔ Relationship-first strategies

These are large, generalized groupings, and specific new starts will often mix elements from each, sprinkle in some new creative ideas, and resist categorization. However, even with its limitations, this sort of broad classification of strategies can be helpful in introducing key strategic themes to those attempting to discover a strategic direction that might work for them.

These strategies are often connected to a discipleship-formation system, so that the first step for people's engagement with the new church is also the preferred first step in their disciple-making process. A typical disciple-making process includes the ways in which someone comes to understand and accept the tenets of Christian beliefs, the ways in which someone comes to adopt and live out the personal and social practices of Christianity, the ways in which someone comes to enlist and participate in Christian community, and the ways in which someone establishes individual relationships among supportive Christian mentors. Each of these generalized church-planting strategies approaches discipleship with a different first step:

Planting Strategy	Step 1	Step 2	Step 3	Step 4
Fellowship-first	Community	Relationship	Practice	Belief
Worship-first	Belief	Practice	Relationship	Community
Discipleship-first	Practice	Community	Belief	Relationship
Relationship-first	Relationship	Community	Practice	Belief

Within these different strategies, ministry context, theological tradition, and leadership preference will create variance among the order of steps two through four. However, looking at first steps and how they relate to discipleship development can provide a helpful overview of planting strategies.

Fellowship-first Strategies

Fellowship-first strategies were popular in the postwar United States. This strategy begins by inviting people to form groups focused on social connections. In the past, this included men's groups, women's groups, couple's dinners, businessmen's Bible studies, youth fellowship groups, or new mothers' luncheons. Churches would often start with renting or building a "fellowship hall" with a kitchen to host these groups. As postwar suburbs grew outward to the outskirts of US cities, people were looking to meet their neighbors and create a new community. As white, middle-class people emptied out of US cities, the remaining city-dwellers yearned to create a new sense of solidarity and interconnection. People were looking to create social connections. The church was seen as a place where you could safely meet people and get involved in your community. Within this approach, disciples were made by first introducing new people to practicing Christians within social groupings. Although rarely stated so bluntly, the approach's motto might have been, "Come meet these people who are friends of Jesus!" When new people began to like the friends of Jesus, then they were invited to become part of the community of Jesus' friends.

The fellowship-first discipling approach might also be described as discipling by osmosis. *Osmosis* is a scientific term for the slow process of assimilating one thing into another. The technical definition of *osmosis* is the movement of solution from a region of greater concentration across a semipermeable membrane to a region of lesser concentration. In this analogy, Christians with a greater concentration of faith pass that faith along to those with less faith through the semipermeable membrane of social connections within the Christian community. Discipleship is grown passively as a natural outgrowth of being part of a community with a higher concentration of Christian disciples. The advantage of this system is that it doesn't take a great effort, training, or intention from faithful Christians to make new disciples. On the other hand, its major shortcomings are that it tends to work only with people who are fairly homogeneous and that it tends to create disciples who are more loyal to their social groups and connections than to Christ. In many ways, when used, this strategy has been more effective at creating "good church people" than it has been at creating deeply committed disciples of Jesus Christ.

Worship-first Strategies

Inspired by Christian camp-meeting traditions, revival worship, and rock 'n' roll concerts, the US baby boomer generation began to develop a different approach to starting new churches that began with worship first. This generation was looking for meaning and purpose, for something spiritual and worthy of trust and awe. New churches adapted to this changing spiritual quest by prioritizing an inspiring, engaging, and uplifting experience of worship. New churches began with renting or building auditoriums with stages that were big enough for musicians with drums, guitars, amplifiers, and keyboards. Lighting, sound, and video eventually became as important as the preaching to an immersive experience. New churches were started as a partnership between the preaching pastor and the worship-leading musician. With a great worship experience, new churches could attract a crowd of believers and potential new converts.

This discipleship strategy's goal was for individuals to have a personal encounter with God. New people were invited to come to worship as their first experience of church. Through the music, preaching, prayers, and invitation to discipleship, the worship service focused on inspiring and encouraging individuals to have an emotive experience of God's love and grace. The large-group nature of this experience allowed for a certain level of anonymity for individual worshipers, as they could get lost in a crowd. New churches invested heavily in marketing efforts to ensure a critical mass of worshipers at the launch service in order to provide the energy and anonymity necessary for this approach. Although worship happened in large groups, discipleship was essentially a personal and individual relationship with God.

This approach was especially effective in helping create new disciples and first-time faith commitments. However, it often struggled with methods of growing more mature disciples and disciple-making communities. Over time, the emphasis on more and more spectacular worship experiences has become prohibitively expensive. New churches in this model need a great deal of financial support if they are going to create the necessarily memorable worship experiences.

The focus on personal experiences also created a somewhat individualistic approach to faith, with little connection or investment in a faith community. This individualism eventually gave rise to a consumeristic "church-shopping" culture, where Christians move from church to church looking for the best worship, the best preaching, or the best children's ministries. As new and existing churches have competed with one another, the few most-attractive churches have grown larger as the many less-attractive churches have grown smaller. Even while a few churches have grown very large, in general this has led to a substantial decrease in the number of churchgoers and professed Christians in the United States.

Discipleship-first Strategies

As they experienced the limits of attractional, worship-first strategies, new church planters in the United States began exploring alternative approaches. As they began to see themselves as part of post-Christian cultures, the planters drew inspiration from the work of missionaries to create a missional approach to starting new churches. They recalled the past successful missionary movements among the Methodists in North America, and they researched the thriving missionary movements in contemporary Africa and Asia. This more missional approach begins with the invitation to join in the practices of Christian discipleship, especially acts of compassion and devotion. Church planters are sent by God on a mission to a specific group of people. They begin by meeting and, often, living among the people they hope to serve. The planter listens to the needs of their people and begins helping find ways to meet their needs. This often takes the form of direct services to the community through compassionate ministries such as literacy programs, immigration legal services, recovery groups, establishing low-income housing, food ministries, marriage-support counseling, or employment training. This strategy depends on Christians engaging communities with love, compassion, and practical assistance. These practices of compassion inspire new people to ask questions about the motivations of the Christian missionaries. In response to these questions, new people are invited to join in helping with these acts of compassion and are welcomed into the accompanying group-devotional practices. In this way, new believers see discipleship modeled and are invited to join in the lifestyle practice of Christian discipleship even before they have ever attended a worship service or given assent to a set of Christian beliefs. The missional community of practice is the center of invitation, and new churches grow organically from the multiplication of these missional communities.

With its focus on discipleship practices, this approach to church planting takes longer to initiate new disciples, but those new disciples are often more committed to their faith and their faith community. Starting with discipleship is designed to have greater success in making new disciples among people who are unfamiliar with Christian faith and is likely a more appropriate strategy among the increasingly non-Christian populations of people in the United States. This strategy, however, takes time to develop. Identifying and relieving a real community need as a witness to God's love consumes a lot of time and resources. There can be a long period of time between inviting inquiring people into a community of practice and those new people supporting the ministries of compassion. Church planters have to be patient, and it can take a lot of outside financial investment to pay a professional clergyperson for the length of time it takes to develop a self-sustaining financial model. This strategy is much more successful among bivocational or non-paid church planters.

Given the tightly formed missional community, the greatest hurdle for this strategy is multiplying out from the initial founding group. Too often, these new churches don't expand beyond a single-cell community of direct, interpersonal relationships among a relatively small group of people. Embedding the expectation of growth and multiplication takes intentional effort and vision-casting from the planter and core church leaders. They must always be radiating outward the expanding love of God or risk the community closing into itself through the gravity of its own satisfactory relationships. When they can accomplish this, however, the groups have the capacity to multiply exponentially.

Because it derives its inspiration and methodology from missionary activities, this discipleship-first approach can often fall victim to the colonial power dynamics of past missionary activities. Missionaries are not universally viewed as helpful by the people they hoped to serve, and some missionaries have been terribly destructive. As church planters are "sent" on mission from someplace else, they are usually outsiders. It takes tremendous self-awareness and cross-cultural gifting for planters to avoid bringing with them their own cultural bias and preferences. Too often, missionary planters confuse cultural expressions of church with essentials of Christian faith. In their confusion, they can seek to transform a community's culture instead of offering them a faith that adapts and grows within that culture. In addition, a "sent" missionary often has access to greater financial and power resources than do the people they are serving. This sets up an inequality that can undermine the development of a church. An unhelpful byproduct of this imbalance has been the emergence of relatively authoritarian leaders who control and direct the lives of the people in their congregations. Without intentional efforts to oppose them, these colonial temptations can undermine the core efforts of effective witness through mercy, compassion, and devotion, resulting in a collapse of this strategy.

Relationship-first Strategies

Relationship-first strategies have risen from within the discipleship-first strategies of missional church planting. Instead of beginning with acts of compassionate witness, this strategy attempts to begin with authentic and mutual individual relationships. The church planter begins with deep listening through dozens and dozens of one-on-one conversations and encounters. The goal is to have people feel that they are fully and deeply heard as an act of incarnating the individual attention of a loving God.

Individual listening is in itself seen as an act of witness and hospitality. The planter, through individual relationships, coaches and curates a web of direct relationships among people. As the relationship network grows, the planter focuses on cultivating people with many relationship connections who serve as network nodes. Instead of removing people from their existing relationship networks and reforming them into a new church-relationship network, Christian faith is spread one-on-one within the existing relationships of the community. In practice, this happens through listening, dialogue, conversation, care, encouragement, and challenge between two people in direct relationship. These relationships are characterized by mutual vulnerability, where both people are open to growth and transformation. As the relationship networks grow, interested people are invited into Christian practices and to form larger groups for shared practice and faith development. Over time, this can transform entire communities, as more and more people begin living as Christian disciples while staying interconnected within their non-Christian relationship networks.

This planting strategy attempts to avoid the colonial impulses of the missional, discipleship-first strategy, but it can be very difficult to scale beyond the initial relationship network of the planter. It requires a simple and powerful distillation of Christian faith that can be set free to transform the faith of people in a culturally engaging way. It also requires great patience and emotional intelligence from the planter, who may not see many measurable metrics of success. If you don't want people to "come to church" but, instead, want them to "be church" for the people in their lives, you won't be able to use attendance or participation numbers as a primary growth metric. Because measuring fruitfulness is hard, existing church and denominational leaders can struggle to see this as an effective strategy.

This is still an emerging strategy in the United States, and it may or may not develop more fully among its practitioners. The relationship-first strategy is easily susceptible to syncretism as its gospel message is passed from one person directly to another; like the children's game of Telephone, the message frequently gets misheard and mishandled in transmission. With the overwhelming interference of societal messages of consumerism, nationalism, racism, sexism, classism, and other non-Christian values, the good news of Christ can be easily corrupted and coopted. More than other approaches, this strategy decentralizes religious authority and trusts the Holy Spirit to guide the priesthood of all believers. This makes it both more adaptable to quickly changing ministry contexts and more susceptible to individual and cultural influences.

Discerning a Strategy

Strategies for starting new churches grow directly out of the intersection of the calling, vision, and gifts of the planter with the culture, needs, and habits of the community. In some settings, the key planting leader will be working with a team who will help to discern and refine this calling, this vision, and these gifts. In other settings, the planter might be working through these elements on his or her own. In all cases, strategy is entirely contextual. The surest path to discouragement and failure is to unreflectively adopt someone else's strategy and try to replicate it in an entirely different context with different leaders. Curtis has been part of planting three different congregations. Each one required different strategies, different methods, and different approaches, even when they shared common leaders and relatively similar population demographics. Discernment of an appropriate strategy requires deep theological self-reflection on the part of the planter as well as comprehensive understanding of the ministry context. The rest of this section will explore the personal discernment journey of the planter, while exploration of the ministry context will be treated more fully in the later chapter on "Where to Plant?"

Discernment is the process of discovering God's direction and guidance. For church planting, this discernment is framed by two faith statements; both Curtis and Bener have seen these play out multiple times in their own ministries. The first faith statement is the belief that God does not call those whom God does not equip; when a planter hears and understands a calling from God to a specific ministry, God will be faithful in equipping that planter with the gifts and resources that person needs to succeed at God's mission. The first problem here, however, is that sometimes a planter will incorrectly discern a call. Mistakes do happen, even when people feel entirely sure of a calling from God, and even good-hearted people can have their vision clouded by unintentional bias. There always seem to be plenty of church planters called to start new churches in suburbs with good school systems, but finding those called to serve communities of poverty and scarcity always seems to be more difficult. And the second problem is that God's mission is not always our mission. Planters want to change the world, make disciples, and herald the arrival of the reign of God. However, sometimes God has different missions in mind. Sometimes God's mission is to prepare the way for something else, to struggle and witness to God's steadfast faithfulness, or to be a humble witness without much honor in the eyes of other people. Both of these problems can make discernment of a call difficult to see in the midst of planting a new church, even if it might be clearer in retrospect.

The second faith statement is that the Holy Spirit can guide through giftedness. In some ways, this is the mirror image of the first statement, and it is God's help for those of us who need assistance in discerning a calling. Because God's calling and mission can be difficult to discern, God sends us hints through the gifts, talents, and strengths that God has given through the power of the Holy Spirit. If God is gifting a planter, God intends those gifts to be used. Sometimes we can get guidance as to God's calling by carefully exploring how those gifts, talents, and strengths might be used. This is where planter assessment can be helpful in determining calling, mission, and strategy.

In the planter assessment process, the potential planter engages in a self-examination process and reflects together with a group of trusted planting mentors who provide feedback and alternative perspectives. The planter assessment process is more fully described in the earlier chapter on "Who Is a Planter?" When done correctly, this process can help the planter determine a calling to plant, a preferred planting strategy, and a personal planting vision. An integral part of the assessment process is "counting the cost," when the potential planter explores his or her personal commitment to the risks of starting a new church or faith community. While doing this, potential planters are often asked to explore and articulate their sense of calling to start a new church. The call statement is reviewed and evaluated by the assessment team. For some potential planters, this is the moment when they confirm their call, while others discern at this point that they aren't called at all. This call statement provides a theological grounding for discerning a strategy.

Also, during the assessment process, potential planters learn about their gifts, talents, and strengths for ministry. These can be helpful in thinking through strategies. A planter with a lot of gifts and strengths in forming relationships might be better served with a relationship-first strategy, while a planter who is an excellent preacher and communicator might consider a worship-first strategy. Strategies should play to the planter's strengths. Entrepreneurship can be a hard journey, and planting a new church or faith community is one of the more difficult kinds of entrepreneurial efforts. Working in ways that rely upon a planter's strengths will increase the overall effectiveness and productivity of the planter's efforts, slightly easing the demands.

Finally, the assessment process can help potential planters name a personal vision for what they hope to achieve through starting a new church or faith community. This vision describes the reality that they hope to emerge through their planting work. A vision must be big enough that it requires the planter to rely on God's help, otherwise it won't be sufficiently mobilizing to the planter or to potential participants. Curtis uses three evaluative questions to determine whether the vision is big enough:

1. **Is it world-changing?** Will the world be changed to better reflect the reign of God? Will anyone notice the change? Will anyone care?

2. **Is it life-altering?** Will people's lives be different in a good way? Will hearts, minds, and souls be transformed? Will it deal with matters of fundamental concern?

3. **Is it worthy of sacrifice?** Will it be worth the investment of time, money, and life? Will it be the worth the cost, even if it costs us our lives?

This vision, when wrestled out with faithful seeking, can give direction to the appropriate strategy. Some planting strategies lead more easily toward making many new disciples. Other strategies lead more easily toward making more-committed disciples. Depending upon the planter's personal vision, one strategy might be more appropriate than another.

Building a Strategy

With direction through the process of discernment, the next step is to build a planting strategy. This strategy leans on the planter's strengths and is rooted in the contextual realities of the people being served by the new church or faith community. A strategy can be built in several different ways. For years, Curtis coached planters through a process of vision and mission-statement generation, followed by setting annual goals and quarterly benchmarks that were strategic, measurable, achievable, resourced, and timed (SMART goals). This process often involved using large sheets of paper and dozens of sticky notes in a retreat setting. More recently, however, Curtis has shifted to using a start-up canvas model. (The people at https://www.oratio.co/innovation have a nicely thought-out model that works for a variety of new kinds of spiritual entrepreneurs and ministry ventures.) A start-up canvas asks a series of specific questions that help to describe the fundamentals of a new enterprise, such as

- What is the value proposition? What value will this new ministry bring to the participants? What is the need people experience, and how will it be met by this ministry?
- What kinds of relationships will you develop with participants?
- What activities and resources are necessary to provide the value proposition through this ministry?
- How will you generate and spend revenue to support this ministry?
- Who are your key partners, and who are your potential participants?

Regardless of the template that is used, it is important to write out a strategy. The activity of writing out a strategy document forces a planter to consider all the details of the plan.

This is not, however, a one-time process. The strategy will need to be continuously evaluated and revised. Typically, working together with other leaders in the new ministry, coaches, consultants, and denominational leaders, the planter will rewrite the strategy several times within the first year. The planter writes out an initial strategy during discernment and planning time. Usually, this is the strategy document that is provided to denominational permission-giving authorities or to potential funding and resource partners. After the planter begins working the strategy within the specific community context, he or she will need to rewrite significant portions of the strategy to account for the realities of the particular mission field. The next rewrite comes when the planter has assembled a team of other leaders who are partnering to start the new ministry. The gifts, strengths, and calling of this leadership team will open up new strategic directions and cause the abandonment of others. The next significant rewrite typically happens after the first few public events, where actual participant feedback allows for testing of core assumptions about the ministry's value and capacity to engage real people in that specific community.

Strategy is important—but hold it lightly. The most important step in any strategy is *the next step*. After taking that step forward, the horizon changes—and so may the best path toward the destination.

7

How Leads to What

"You will receive power when the Holy Spirit has come
upon you; and you will be my witnesses in Jerusalem,
in all Judea and Samaria, and to the ends of the earth."
—ACTS 1:8

Since its public emergence in the early part of 2020, the COVID-19
pandemic has had a significant impact upon the activity of church planting globally compared to the activity before the coronavirus crisis hit the
world. Notably, many church-planting organizations in the United States
and in other countries around the globe find it overwhelming to carry on
with the task of starting new churches during this time of uncertainty.
Other troubling crises such as violence, systemic racism, economic melt-
down, and more have decelerated the efforts of sustaining the flourishing
of new church development in most parts of the world.

And yet, even amid the coronavirus pandemic, we hear and see
incredible stories of how God's people in new faith communities are
experiencing a deepening of their relationship with God and their fellowship with other followers of Christ. For such a time as this, while nations
and communities are dealing with these worrying crises, God is actively

working with faith communities who are extending welcome, hospitality, and inclusion to all God's people.

We see an increase in a variety of models of new faith communities or new ministries emerging amid these uncertain times. Church planters are using innovative strategies to gather and engage a group of people in deepening their faith experience through worship, discipleship, and other essential ministries of a faith community or local church. And more of these new followers of Jesus are growing, maturing, and participating in bringing about both change in people's lives and transformation within their local neighborhoods and society in general. Starting new churches, indeed, is one of the most effective ways to fulfill the mission of making disciples of Jesus Christ, who then become active partners in accomplishing God's plan of transforming the world with the love of God.

Planter Story: Jasper Peters and Belong Church

Belong Church in Denver, Colorado, is one of these faith communities— a model of a new church that fully embraces and puts into practice the values of diversity, inclusion, and justice in everything that they do as a new church. In chapter 5, we learned that the gifts, strengths, and experiences of church planters determine the type of new church or faith community that will emerge. We found this to be accurate at The Gathering in Virginia Beach with Rachel Gilmore, and we also found this to be the case at the Belong Church in Denver, with Jasper Peters as their lead planter.

Who is Jasper Peters? His parents, who were both active in the US civil rights movement, raised Jasper and his siblings to be deeply rooted in what it means to be Black in America. Their Black church experience also shaped Jasper's faith and self-understanding as a Black person. Jasper recalls,

> So, I am a Black Baptist kid going into a Catholic school in a white and mostly Jewish neighborhood. I am the only Black student in my entire class all through elementary. There was no way for me to share most of my experiences, like my church experience, with other kids, because they will not get it; and the kids that can

relate with my life experiences are not there, for they are
in different places.

In this particular neighborhood, both Jasper's faith tradition as a Baptist
and his life experience as a Black person made him feel like there was no
place for him. He says, "So much of my formative years was spent in the
context where I felt I was alone or didn't really have a home."

As a young adult, Jasper responded to the call to enter into full-time
Christian ministry in The United Methodist Church. After his short
tenure as an associate pastor at Trinity United Methodist Church, his
district superintendent appointed him to plant a new church in the city
of Denver, Colorado. Jasper recalls that his initial response was, "I'm not
equipped to do this, and I don't yet feel called to church planting. But I
am willing to learn more." He went to the Exponential Church Planting
event, where he met a group of his fellow United Methodist church planters and was introduced to Path 1—a church planting initiative operated
by The United Methodist Church. In Jasper's conversations with fellow
United Methodists, together, they came up with a clear understanding
as to why they were called to plant new churches. Jasper remembered a
transformative moment of conversation when he began to understand a
calling to plant a new faith community, along with the questions he and
his fellow participants were asking themselves:

> What if Jesus was serious about this idea of God's king-
> dom? What if Jesus was not just [being] hyperbolic or
> metaphorical when he talked about this idea of the reign
> of God? What if this radical version of reality called
> "kingdom of God" was actually a real thing that we are
> supposed to chase after? What would the world really be
> like if the last would be first? What would happen to the
> world and the church if we are really pursuing this Jesus
> movement? We responded in one accord: The church
> would be diverse, inclusive, and justice-oriented. We are
> called to be a community that takes this whole God's
> kingdom seriously [the way] Jesus did it.

Jasper responded to the call to plant a new church—the Belong
Church—that is grounded in both his faith and life experience as a Black

person and centered in the Jesus movement of building God's kingdom in a way that is diverse, inclusive, and justice-oriented. The strategies that Jasper and his planting team used in gathering people at Belong Church are grounded in these core values. Thus, Belong Church emerges as a community of faith that is committed to the vision of God's reign, where every person in the fellowship can feel at home and make a difference in the world.

The strategies used to gather and inspire a group of people into discipleship will shape the model of the new church or new ministry. Whether it is a parachute drop, a multisite campus, a church within a church, a fresh expression, a spiritual entrepreneurship, or a restart, the model of organization emerges from the strategies and practices used by the planting leader or leaders. By exploring the strategies Jasper followed in planting Belong, we can learn how those strategies impact the models of new faith community used in starting and shaping Belong as a diverse, inclusive, justice-oriented faith community.

1.   **Take the vision of God's kingdom seriously.** This is what the Belong Church aims at being: a church that practices the vision and values of what it means to be a God's-kingdom community. The Belong Church stands firmly in solidarity with LGBTQIA+ and other marginalized people in the community. They hope that other churches will also clearly articulate their stand on being an inclusive church. According to Jasper, "The grace and love of God is meaningless if we make it conditional. So, what [would] it mean if we never questioned the belovedness of the people who walked in through our doors?" Being a diverse church is what makes Belong Church unique in many ways. The core leadership of this new faith community are people who have experienced marginalization within American society in general—and within the American church specifically—because of their theology, color of skin, language, sexual orientation, gender expression, or life. These are the people who are the foundation, the backbone, of this new church. Jasper knew how it felt to be alone. At the core of his strategy in gathering people, he has been consistently asking this question: What does it mean for the church to be diverse? According to Jasper,

What if the ways in which we are different are not a liability that we should sort of smooth over or ignore, but what if it is actually a gift? What if God has given us this gift to help build up the church and bless the world?

Being a church that is justice-oriented means, as Jasper explains, "The gospel calls us to actual transformation, not just to make us feel good." Belong Church is committed to and intentional about articulating and practicing what it means to work together for justice, especially through movements of social transformation such as the movement for Black Lives Matter. They are absolutely committed to helping their people make that deeper connection between what it means to be a disciple of Jesus and what it means to be antiracist. As Jasper says, "I help my people to see [that] those things are so the same." The efforts of inviting and gathering people around this vision of being a God's-kingdom community follow the strategy of Jesus. A community engagement grounded upon these values can be useful and can bear fruit only if there is high commitment, intentionality, and seriousness among the church's leadership.

2. **Understand that church is a gift to the world.** Being bold and more explicit about their antiracist expression of their discipleship would not have been the Belong Church's reality as a community of faith if they hadn't chosen to strengthen their strategies in building up a church around those core values of diversity, inclusion, and justice, which also paved the way for creating a church that acts as a representative of the vision of God's kingdom. They are able to position the church on the side of freedom, justice, and equality during this time in history because of their self-understanding of the church itself as a part of God's gift to the world. According to Jasper,

> We are in a place now where we can be actively antiracist. I wear my "Black Lives Matter" shirt in the pulpit, and no one blinks an eye. It's not a problem for people. We are studying about antiracism, and we're dealing with it, and we're having hard conversations between Black people and white people. And they're working it

out, and they're figuring out how to be and build a loving community.

Jasper's strategy of nurturing and building up Belong Church as a gift to the world also helped facilitate the creation of a model of a new church that aims to serve as a foretaste of God's kingdom, here and now. In a wonderful way, this move enables the Belong Church to serve as a visible sign of God's reign. For such a time as this, this new church is fully and boldly living its vision and identity as a model of God's kingdom community. According to Jasper,

> More than 95 percent of folks in [our] church have never been involved with The United Methodist Church before coming to Belong. They know very little about their mother church, and yet, they fully embraced this conviction that they are called to be a gift to The United Methodist Church.

3. **Perform deep practices of authentic conversations and building relationships.** As Jasper puts it,

> The church that we want to be is a relational church that is built and made by actually just being in relationship with people and being willing to be honest about what's important and what your priorities are and what your dreams are.

Using this honest-to-goodness, authentic approach is not about what the new church thinks or says is good, thus pretending that they have everything figured out and that they are the "savior of the world"; instead, it is more about being able to gather people who have been searching for a faith community that is real, authentic, and caring. Being authentic in conversations with people to build lasting relationships with them, says Jasper, requires a "willingness to be who we say we're trying to be and the courage to let people in the community know who we are trying to be as a church." Like any successful church planter, Jasper worked with his team in creating a culture within the church that models this strategy of authentic conversations and building relationships. He spent extensive time with the members of his planting team, listening to them and hearing their stories, affirming and building them up. From the beginning of this new church, the responsibility for caring for one another in deep and significant ways has been a practice that they have tried to live out among themselves, as well as with people whom they encounter in the community.

It is worth lifting up some of the comments from Jasper about when he has had these sorts of authentic conversations with different kinds of people and the impact they have had upon him both as a person and as a lead planter. Jasper describes some of the early relational interactions:

> The thing that I didn't realize before doing all of this was how to go from four people to more than that: [It] is by literally talking to everyone that I know. By having these conversations with every person that I could get ahold of who is willing to talk to me about this. Sometimes it was doing things that were very obviously convenient. . . . But sometimes it was doing things that were not convenient. . . . There were moments that had me out of my comfort zone.

In planting a new faith community, where you are talking to a lot of different kinds of people and inviting people to check this new thing out, there are critical strategies that need to be carried out with absolute authenticity. Jasper and his team have always tried to do their best in practicing authenticity, and now more people are finding this church to be their own community where they feel they belong.

Jasper demonstrated this approach by modeling it with his team. He didn't just talk about the importance of it and about how to practice this approach with his group of leaders but also modeled it by example. While talking with his leaders about the importance of spending intentional time with people, learning their stories, and being authentically present, it surely helps them to catch the concept and the reason why it is important for their ministry. However, when they themselves actually experience how Jasper intentionally spends time with others by listening, interacting, and relating with integrity and authenticity, that's when they really get excited to go out and meet with people in the same way they are experiencing at Belong Church. People follow the leaders they know and trust—leaders who walk the walk and never ask anyone to do something they are not willing to model themselves. Jasper's strategies are the byproducts of his faith and life experiences, and that is the reason why these strategies work very well for this new church.

Jasper's rootedness in his history and culture as a Black person made him a great fit to lead a church like Belong Church, especially in such a period of history as this, where the people of the United States are struggling to live together as one human race and build a nation together where no one would be cast out simply because of their skin color or their perspective on what is good for the life and future of the nation. Jasper's life and faith experiences as a Black man have prepared him to invite others to join him in building a faith community where people can be free to share their stories and to listen to and learn from others. It is inspiring to know from Jasper's story that his strategies in organizing and sustaining this church were not learned simply from textbooks or PowerPoint presentations. Rather, they have been informed, vetted, and motivated by his own faith, history, and life experiences as a beloved child of God. It is no wonder why Belong Church is a home for Jasper and for all kinds of people: Its doors are wide open to all God's children who are seeking a home for themselves. Jasper's journey from his early years growing up to leading the formation of Belong Church is a testimony that God is still in the business of creating a community of faith where all God's people can call and claim it as their home. Jasper had actually experienced what it meant to be invisible, ignored, and alone. But he has broken down the walls and claimed his belovedness throughout his life, which is especially important during this time when he is leading a new church that aims to live out what it means to be a sign of God's reign in the world.

Church planting is hard work. When you are in the middle of what is going on in the church plant, it is exciting for the most part but frightening at the same time, just like riding a roller coaster. It brings unspeakable joy, especially when changes are happening in the lives of people, and even greater joy when the collective work of the church brings about transformation in the community and society in a powerful way. Belong Church is a diverse, inclusive, and justice-oriented United Methodist congregation—a community of faith that intentionally invites, welcomes, gathers, equips, and unleashes its people to make a difference. They do it as their special gift and contribution to God's mission as partners in building God's kingdom for the sake of all God's people and the whole creation. Although it can be hard to start a new church, Jasper recalls,

> You don't have to live in fear of failure or rejection, because no matter what happens, you're never, ever in this alone. And you have to understand the gifts that God has given you and the gifts of people around you.

In this chapter, we learned the importance of having clarity around the strategies of starting a new faith community and how doing so helps shape the model of what a new church will look like. Drawing from the gifts, strengths, and life experiences of the church planter and the planting team also plays a significant role in nurturing and sustaining this model of a new church or faith community. In Belong Church, the church planter and the planting team are intentional in shaping the culture and directions of their church by maintaining a proper balance of applying relevant strategies on the one hand and flavoring them with the faith and life experiences of everyone in the church on the other. Thus, we see a new church that embodies the vision and values of a beloved community. We celebrate this new church for their being and becoming an expression of the reign of God.

In the next chapter, we will discuss the different models for new churches, new faith communities, and new ministries.

8

What Is a New Faith Community?

When the day of Pentecost had come, they were all together in one place. And suddenly from heaven there came a sound like the rush of a violent wind, and it filled the entire house where they were sitting. Divided tongues, as of fire, appeared among them, and a tongue rested on each of them. All of them were filled with the Holy Spirit and began to speak in other languages, as the Spirit gave them ability.

—Acts 2:1-4

When people start a new gathering of worshiping, discipling, and witnessing Christians, there can be a lot of debate about what to call it. Is it a church? Is it a faith community? Is it a fellowship of believers? Is it a ministry? Is it something else? Throughout this book, we've interchangeably used the labels of *church*, *faith community*, and *ministry* to help potential planters see themselves in this resource regardless of which label they prefer. In general, people tend to use the label of "ministry" to describe a subgroup of a larger established church, "faith community" as a smaller or semiautonomous gathering, and "church" as a standalone larger congrega-tion. In many ways, these labels are insignificant to the people involved in the new group. They are much more concerned about encountering a loving and living God through the grace and promise of Jesus Christ in a community shaped and inspired by the Holy Spirit.

In essence, all of these are simply different forms and expressions of church. Church, as a gathering of disciples of Jesus or congregation of believers (*ecclesia* or "gathering"), is a particularly Christian idea that developed from the traditional Jewish idea of synagogue. Synagogues were regular gatherings of Jews to read, discuss, and learn from a teacher or rabbi. With the destruction of the first Jerusalem Temple and the Babylonian Exile, synagogues became more prominent and served as a second focus of Jewish identity alongside the rebuilt Temple during late antiquity. During his lifetime, Jesus was most often identified as a rabbi by his Jewish contemporaries, and it is likely that his original followers were thought of as a sort of traveling synagogue. Both *synagogue* and *church* have linguistic roots in the image of a people summoned or "called out" by God to gather or assemble.

A new church, then, is any gathering of Christians and seekers. In practice, Curtis often looks for three behaviors that mark a new church:

1. **Worship**—Does the community join in prayer, praise, and group learning?
2. **Discipleship**—Does the community invite seekers to begin their journey of following Christ, and do believers continue to mature in their faith?
3. **Service**—Does the community witness to their neighbors through acts of compassion, mercy, and justice and make tangible the love of Christ?

Curtis once worked with a group of people in rural New England who had *accidentally* started a new church. A church in one town owned a former parsonage that was located in a different town, several miles away. The church was not using the parsonage, but a few of the people in the town in which it was located asked if they could use it to serve a free community meal once a week. This seemed like a good idea, and so the community meal initiative got started. After a few months, some of the people coming to the meal asked if they could stay after the meal for prayer, singing, and a devotion time. One of the lay leaders of the other church agreed to come over and lead them, so they began. This time of worship gave birth to a couple of small Bible studies that volunteers led during the week in the old parsonage. New people kept coming to the meal and the worship service, and in the next year, they celebrated their first two baptisms. Were they worshiping, discipling, and serving? Yes. Without really planning to do so, they had started a new church.

New Testament New Church Planting

The New Testament has a very simple view of church that puts Christ's presence at the center of a gathering of interrelated believers, seekers, and disciples. This basic description seems to allow for a wide variety of formal structures or models. The primary time that Jesus uses the word *church* reinforces this idea of the church as a gathering of Christians or as the called-out assembly of God's people centered on Christ. In Matthew 16:18, Jesus responds to Peter's declaration that Jesus is the Messiah by proclaiming, "And I tell you, you are Peter, and on this rock I will build my church, and the gates of Hades will not prevail against it." Of significance is the idea that Jesus is the one who will build the church, not Peter or the other disciples. The church is to be called into existence by Jesus himself. Jesus provides a harvest metaphor for this work of God in the parable of the growing seed:

> [Jesus] also said, "The kingdom of God is as if someone would scatter seed on the ground, and would sleep and rise night and day, and the seed would sprout and grow, he does not know how. The earth produces of itself, first the stalk, then the head, then the full grain in the head. But when the grain is ripe, at once he goes in with his sickle, because the harvest has come." (Mark 4:26-29)

In expanding God's reign in the world, people have a part in the planting and scattering of seed; but it is God who brings the growth, even if the sowers do not understand how.

This cooperation between God and God's people is evident in the commission that Jesus gives his followers at the conclusion of the Gospel of Matthew:

> Jesus came and said to them, "All authority in heaven and on earth has been given to me. Go therefore and make disciples of all nations, baptizing them in the name of the Father and of the Son and of the Holy Spirit, and teaching them to obey everything that I have commanded you. And remember, I am with you always, to the end of the age. (28:18-20)

In his commission to them, Jesus gave the disciples the threefold mission of making disciples through baptism, teaching the commandments of Jesus, and remembering the accompaniment of Jesus with his followers throughout the ages. Jesus' followers are not sent all alone into the world with the task of multiplying disciples; rather, Jesus promises to be with them in this work. This passage does not specifically mention forming the newly baptized disciples into churches, but the gathered community seems to naturally and organically emerge from the relationships of the disciples.

This theme of cooperation between God and disciples in planting new churches is continued in the description of the community of believers in Acts 2:43-47. Following the revelation of the Holy Spirit through Peter and the disciples at Pentecost, we read of the believers being together and having all things in common, and how, "Day by day the Lord added to their number those who were being saved" (Acts 2:47). This is also seen as God's work, not simply the work of the apostles.

The apostle Paul embraces this concept and connects it to his mission of starting new churches. In response to the divisions in the newly formed Corinthian church, he writes to them, "I planted, Apollos watered, but God gave the growth. So neither the one who plants nor the one who waters is anything, but only God who gives the growth" (1 Cor. 3:6-7). He insists in 1 Corinthians 1:12-17 that none of the churches "belong" to him; instead, they are all undivided in Christ, who is the primary founder of each church community. Paul emphasizes that it is God's power that leads to new converts, not Paul's eloquence or cleverness:

> When I came to you, brothers and sisters, I did not come
> proclaiming the mystery of God to you in lofty words
> or wisdom. For I decided to know nothing among you
> except Jesus Christ, and him crucified . . . so that your
> faith might rest not on human wisdom but on the power
> of God. (1 Cor. 2:1-2, 5)

Paul's key strategy for planting new churches was to emphasize the power of God at work in relationship with people. He seemed to value relationships with others and worked almost exclusively with a partner or team in every place he visited. He would usually begin by visiting the local synagogue with his companions, as seen in Acts 13:13-52. In other communities, he would visit a place where people were gathered for spiritual conversation or for prayer. In Athens (see Acts 17:17-19), Paul starts in the synagogue, then the marketplace, and then is taken to the Areopagus for debate. In Philippi, Paul goes down to the river to "a place of prayer" (Acts 16:13), where he converses with the women gathered there, including Lydia, who would host the church in Philippi and become a Christian leader herself (see vv. 14-15). In each place, Paul would establish a few relationships with local residents. In Acts 18:7-11, Paul, along with Silas and Timothy, raised up conflict in Corinth with their preaching in the synagogue, so they continued teaching and preaching in the house of Titius Justus, where they stayed for a year and a half. The sheer number of women and men who are named as Paul's partners, hosts, patrons, coworkers, leaders, and colleagues tells how important Paul's relationships were in establishing new churches.

Models for New Faith Communities

Given the relative simplicity of the New Testament's definition of *church*, we have seen the evolution of a great variety of types, degrees of autonomy, and models for development of churches and other faith communities. Like variations on a simple musical tune, different planters and contexts will improvise, adapt, and add their own creative spark to the original music. This variation helps us evolve the best launch method to engage a mission field, but it can also be confusing. When is a project a new faith community? When is it a new ministry of an existing church? What's the difference?

Further complication arises from the simple fact that our plans don't always progress the way we expect. A new faith community planted as an autonomous "parachute-drop" church might be adopted by an existing congregation and become an alternative worship service. A young-adult ministry might grow and evolve into a new, independent congregation. Both projects can be fulfilling their missions, but they have changed into something unexpected. When does a project become a new faith community? When does it cease being a new faith community?

To help develop a typology of the different models of new faith communities, we will look at five key areas of autonomy to define a new faith community. These areas are as follows:

1. **Worship**—Does the new faith community regularly meet independently for worship? Does it meet in a different location from any partnering or sponsoring congregations? Does it use a separate staff, style, planning, or language? Does it consist of a different group of people from those who participate in the partner, connected, or sponsoring congregations?

2. **Disciple-making Systems**—Does the new faith community have independent invitation and evangelism practices? Does it have its own small groups, classes, or discipleship programs? Does it offer a unique style of making disciples that fits the people it is trying to reach?

3. **Mission-field Engagement**—Does the new faith community have its own strategy and actions for reaching out to its mission field? Is its mission field defined differently than its partner congregations' mission fields? Does it take independent leadership in connectional efforts to serve its community?

4. **Administration and Finances**—Does the new faith community have its own boards and committees? Does it practice separate collection and management of financial gifts? Does it have its own state and federal nonprofit identification? Is it financially self-sustaining?

5. **Leadership**—Does the new faith community have its own pastoral and lay leadership? Does it have separately assigned staff?

Does it raise up and train its own internal leadership whose primary commitment is to the new faith community?

The Gray Zone

New faith communities are easy to classify at the edges of autonomy, but projects in "the Gray Zone" often need a somewhat more nuanced description. We easily understand that a new worship service is not a new faith community, but what about a new ethnic fellowship that meets separately for worship? On our scale of autonomy, the middle two sections are often the most difficult to characterize as new faith communities within "the Gray Zone." They have some levels of autonomy, but they are also dependent on their partners and sponsors.

Some Types of Ministries That Are Probably Not New Faith Communities

At the lower end of autonomy are new ministries that we recognize are probably not new faith communities. These are incredibly important and valuable expressions of church, and they can be some of the most important arenas for discipleship development. However, they often do not have self-sustaining resources or capacity for multiplication without a relationship with a larger, more autonomous church or organization.

Small-Group Ministry

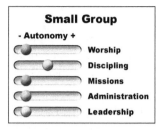

Many churches have small-group ministries that gather people for intentional discipleship. These groups depend on an established church for leadership training, worship opportunities, coordinated missions, and support. Often, these groups are part of a larger disciple-making system within the sponsoring congregation.

Fellowship Group in a Church

Usually involving groups of twenty to fifty participants, these groups (divided into different categories such as men, women, or youth) gather similar kinds of people together for shared discipleship and missions. While they often have unique approaches to discipleship, these groups usually don't meet for their own regular worship and instead are a full part of the larger congregation's leadership and worship experiences.

Alternative or Second Worship Services

Some churches have more than one style or one designated time for worship. These are not typically new faith communities. They share leadership, discipleship, missions, and administration with the larger church. Some may eventually grow into new faith communities with the addition of discipling, mission, and leadership systems.

Some Types of Ministries That Could Be New Faith Communities

In this middle range of autonomy, some of these ministries might be new faith communities, while others might be ministries of a sponsoring congregation or other religious organization. These are often hybrids of dependency and autonomy. One helpful way to classify these is to look at their trajectory. If the new faith community is growing more autonomous, treat it more like a self-sustaining new congregation. If it is stable or growing less autonomous, treat it like a part of its partner churches or sponsoring organizations.

Satellite, Second, or Video Campus

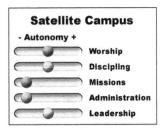

To reach another geography or to multiply worship space or times, a healthy church might launch another campus for worship and discipleship. Sometimes this will include campus-specific leaders, but it is almost always deeply integrated with the sponsoring church's internal culture, vision, and senior leadership. Sometimes a growing church will "adopt" a neighboring church's facility as a site for a satellite campus. In this case, new leadership is almost always placed at the new campus.

New Church Within a Church

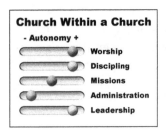

To reach a new group of people, a church might host or launch a congregation that conducts worship and discipling in a profoundly different way with different leadership and a different culture. Sometimes, they will share some missions and depend on each other for administrative, financial, or facilities support. These new faith communities are often targeted for people of new ethnic or language groups or they are designed for people of a different generation than that of the sponsoring congregation.

Satellite Congregation

Different from a satellite campus, a satellite congregation will almost always have separate leadership and distinctive worship from the sponsoring church. Often, it has its own discipling system that might parallel the system in the sponsoring church. Satellite congregations are often staffed by their own pastor and leaders who nurture the connection with the sponsoring church's senior leadership.

Ethnic Fellowship

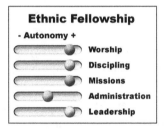

These are often semiautonomous faith communities that meet for their own worship, discipling, and missions with the support of a sponsoring congregation. Often, they will have their own volunteer or paid pastors and leaders, and they will frequently speak a different language or engage in different cultural traditions from their host church. The fellowships will sometimes receive financial support from other congregations or the denomination.

Sponsored, Parented, or Daughter Church

A healthy church might choose to send a group of its members to start a new church in a new location or pursue some other strategy to launch another autonomous congregation by supporting the new church through its launch phase. The goal is an independent congregation, but the new church may continue to relate to senior leadership and receive administrative support from the sponsoring church.

New Faith Enterprise

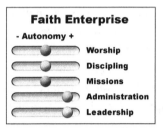

Faith communities are blending with non-profit and for-profit business enterprises. These will often blend community- and relationship-formation activities with other income-generating work to help engage the community and support making disciples. New faith enterprises will vary based on their business models, from church-sponsored schools to restaurants, laundromats, web design, furniture refinishing, brew pubs, or coffee shops.

Intentional or Monastic Communities

Growing in popularity, these are small groups of people who often live together and form intentional spiritual and missional practices to support Christian living. They might have their own worship experiences or participate in a partner congregation's worship. They usually have autonomous lay leadership and sometimes their own clergy.

House or Cell Churches

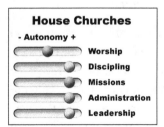

These are small, single-celled churches that meet outside traditional church facilities. Sometimes they have their own clergy through a network of house churches, but they are often lay-led. Sometimes they will share in large worship experiences with a partner church, but many are entirely interconnected networks of small gatherings.

Some Types of Ministries That Are Almost Always New Faith Communities

At the higher end of autonomy and in more traditional church styles, we find planting models that are almost always considered new faith communities. Some of these models may become relatively established without becoming fully self-sustaining. In general, if a ministry has matured beyond the initial decade of being started, it may not be helpful to still continue to treat it as a "new" congregation. Instead, it is probably better to treat it as an established church and normalize its relationships with its sponsors, partners, or denomination in order to make long-term plans for the ministry's ongoing support.

Mission or Supported Church

A mission church is a congregation that is independent in every way, except that it receives ongoing financial support from partner churches or the denomination. Usually, these churches have a mission to serve a population that is financially poor or highly transient and cannot fully fund the mission church's ministry.

Vital Merger Plant

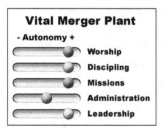

In a vital merger, two or more existing congregations sell their buildings, retire their leadership systems, merge together in a new location, and receive a new pastor trained in church planting. The new church receives its launch funding through the resources of the former congregations. Its goal is not survival but transformation and disciple making in its community. Dirk Elliot has done excellent work providing a theoretical and practical framework for leading this kind of new faith community.[1]

Legacy, Lazarus, or Elijah/Elisha Church Plant

Rather than dying out, an existing congregation may decide to retire and leave its assets as a bequest to a new faith community. A planter and plan are put together, and the ministry of the retiring congregation is celebrated through the launching of a new faith community serving a new group of people.

Adoption of a New Plant

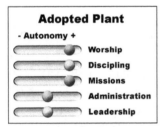

Sometimes, new faith communities are already started and then begin looking for connections and resources through partnerships with another congregation or denomination. This can be a good strategy to reach new ethnic or language groups, but the adopted church needs to take care that it fully understands denominational expectations and organizational culture.

Partnership with a New Plant

Established congregations may partner with a new faith community to provide spiritual, leadership, material, or financial support. Through partnership, the established congregations have a connectional investment in the new faith community, but the new plant remains autonomous in almost every way.

Parachute Drop, Pioneer, or Planter-Driven Plant

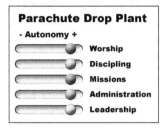

In this model, a planter is "dropped" into a community with little more than a God-given vision for a new faith community. These are very risky and depend on a highly entrepreneurial planter. Because this style of plant is driven exclusively by the planter, it is the most autonomous style of launching a new faith community.

Chartered Church or Organized Charge

This is an established church with its own membership, organization, and representation to its denomination or networks. Even with this high level of autonomy, congregations are still connected through denominational, ecumenical, and geographical relationships for mutual support of their ministries. And all churches are connected together in the body of Christ.

What Is the "Best" Model?

There is no one "best" model for starting a new church. God has used all these models to create world-changing, life-altering communities of Christians. Instead, the model emerges from the gifts of the planter, the strategy of planting, and the available resources. All have benefits, but it can be helpful to think of some of the challenges presented by different models.

Some models can be financially expensive. A parachute-drop start requires several years of outside funding for a paid planter, program staff, and facility rental. A new multisite worship-first venue requires funding for marketing, facility, live-worship leaders, musicians, and full onsite children's ministry. Financially expensive models need a planter who is good at fundraising, financially generous partner churches or denominational funding, and a disciplined launch strategy in order not to run out of funds before the new church is financially self-sustaining.

Some models can be relationally intense. A neo-monastic intentional community where a small group is sharing living quarters requires strong relationship skills and well-defined personal boundaries from the planter. A cell church start that focuses on small, distributed groups requires a planter who can quickly develop and multiply relationships with a large number of leaders. Relationally intensive models demand an emotionally mature planter who is humble enough to allow space for other people to become leaders. They will also need careful support to avoid emotional and relational boundary trespasses, as these models have very intimate relationships that can often enmesh pastoral and personal roles.

Some models are creatively demanding. A new faith enterprise requires leaders who can not only design a disciple-making community but also launch an effective new business enterprise. They must be able to manage the multiplying risks of starting two intertwined ventures simultaneously. A new church within a church demands a vision and a focused knowledge of a different population than those who make up the host congregation. This requires ongoing creative vision and avoiding the subtle pressures to remake the new people to better fit with the culture of the host congregation. Creatively demanding models require planters who are self-motivated, possess high work capacities, and are willing to personally invest in an innovative vision for the new church.

All the models can be spiritually exhausting. Both Curtis and Bener can testify that their time spent starting new churches was among their most challenging, fulfilling, exhausting, and compelling ministries. Planters live every day at the vital intersection of the expanding church and world. They are directly dependent upon the Holy Spirit's power to energize their ministries, as they often have few other resources. They face the regular challenges of pastoring an established church, along with the extraordinary challenges of starting a new ministry. Those that are partnered with existing churches have the benefit of additional resources, but they must also contend with complex and frequently change-resistant relational and organizational systems within their partner churches. Denominational connections can bring additional funding and support, but they come with complex permission-giving systems and multiple levels of supervision that may not all share similar goals or understandings.

All planters must contend with being ambassadors of Christ to a world that hates Christ's message. Christianity is fundamentally countercultural in most societies. Christ preaches love in a world that loves violence. Christ offers gracious forgiveness in societies built on retributive punishment. Christ demands generosity from believers who live in cultures of personal greed and acquisitive accumulation. Christ builds communities across lines of race, gender, nation, or class, even while economies segment people into greater competition for resources. Leaders of established churches experience these same pressures, but they are often able to rely on the support of other Christians within the church. Many planters are initially on their own and spend much of their time among seekers and new believers who are wrestling with the gospel's power to free them from the rulers and idols of the world. The constant demands of representing Christ's values in a hostile world can easily wear down planters. In coaching planters, Curtis and Bener have seen this pressure lead to divorce, unethical practices, depression, and even suicide. Planters and their families need the ongoing support of coaches, spiritual directors, therapists, and prayer intercessors.

Even if being a planter is not your calling, every Christian can offer to support a planter with prayer, encouragement, time, money, and care.

9

What Leads to Where

Do not lie to one another, seeing that you have stripped off the old self with its practices and have clothed yourselves with the new self, which is being renewed in knowledge according to the image of its creator. In that renewal there is no longer Greek and Jew, circumcised and uncircumcised, barbarian, Scythian, slave and free; but Christ is all and in all!

—Colossians 3:9-11

Bener recalls that when he was a child, his father taught his two older sisters how to work a puzzle. They started with one hundred pieces, and the sisters got it done in no time. Completing a one-hundred-piece puzzle easily became a boring task, so they went up to 200 pieces, then 300, and then 500. After every completed puzzle, they became more and more efficient in their approach; they developed skills and strategies on how to complete puzzles with less pressure. Everything quickly changed when they tried to put together a 2,000-piece puzzle that had a very complex pattern. By that point, putting together a puzzle had become more work and less fun. The same can be said about church planting: It is easy until it becomes not-that-easy anymore.

Bener reflects on this memory and his experiences in starting new churches:

> Church planting can be very overwhelming, as I experienced when I led a strategy to plant not just one or two churches but at least sixteen new churches in sixteen municipalities in the whole Province of Cavite in the Philippines. Speaking from my own experience as a church planter, as a local pastor, I led in planting at least seven churches, which was like putting together a 500-piece puzzle. But planting churches in every municipality of an entire province within a six-year period is overwhelming in terms of casting the vision, training leaders, the number of hours spent on planning and evaluation, raising money, and so many other things that are needed to accomplish the mission.
>
> I remember that when I was thirty-three years old and had ten years in full-time service as a local pastor, my bishop in Manila, Bishop Emerito Nacpil, appointed me to serve as district superintendent of churches in the southwestern area of metropolitan Manila. Bishop Nacpil gave me a marching order to launch an aggressive missional strategy that would give birth to a new district in the entire Province of Cavite, southwest of Manila. The strategy was to mobilize all the churches in my district in Manila to plant new churches in Cavite. At that time, I already had seven new churches planted under my leadership, so I was fairly confident in the business of planting new churches. However, the idea of creating a new district in a new mission field was a big challenge. This assignment was much bigger than what I thought I could do as the lead person of such an ambitious project; this was like putting together not a 2,000-piece puzzle but a 5,000-piece puzzle.
>
> My experience in church planting, leadership training, and education in development administration greatly helped me to carry out this mission. It's a challenge to

describe in a few paragraphs everything that happened during this intense work of church planting; it was six years of hard work, planning, executing, and keeping the focus and raising capacity of all the partners in this very progressive ministry-action plan. We accomplished the mission, with fifty-eight churches planted; and a new district was born, with the help of so many church leaders and partners in mission who worked together in birthing Cavite District, which is now a regular annual conference with two established districts. Thanks to God and the hard work of church planters, we put together a 5,000-piece puzzle!

Planter Story: Rodrigo Cruz and The Nett Church

In this section, we will look into the story of The Nett Church—a multi-ethnic, multiracial new church in North Georgia. Rodrigo Cruz shared with us his story of planting this new church, which was like his own version of a 5,000-piece puzzle. It's an amazing story. We hope that sharing his story will point out how the gifts of the planter, the strategies of building a Christian community, and the organizing model all inform the location or target audience for any new ministry, new faith community, or new church. This often includes an analysis of available resources, such as partner churches, people who might be looking for that kind of ministry, supportive permission-giving from other established church leaders or denominations, prayer networks, financial support, facilities, and other materials.

The journey of Rodrigo in birthing and leading The Nett Church started when he felt the call of God for himself and his family to be a part of a multiethnic church movement. Initially, he was hoping to serve as pastor to a local congregation that was racially diverse. However, many of the local churches in his area were homogeneous congregations at the time when he was in discernment about the kind of future ministry God wanted for him. According to Rodrigo,

> The North Georgia Annual Conference [of The United Methodist Church] has more than 900 existing congregations, and most, if not all, of them were racially

specific. There are Black, African American, White, Hispanic, Latino, [and] Asian faith communities. We have all kinds of choices in this conference. [All] of these ethnic churches are homogeneous congregations.

Rodrigo realized from this situation that if he wanted to be appointed to a multiethnic, multiracial faith community, he may as well resolve himself to starting one from scratch. He believes that God put this vision in his heart.

Following the call to plant a multiethnic new faith community, Rodrigo did his diligent work in researching and studying the best location that was ethnically diverse. He found Gwinnett County, a suburban county of Atlanta that is known for being the most diverse county in the southeastern section of the United States. After spending sufficient time surveying this county, Rodrigo approached his district superintendent and other key leaders from the conference to support the vision of starting a multiethnic church in Gwinnett County. With their support, Rodrigo and his wife, Kelly, along with their children, moved to Gwinnett County in 2015. Both Rodrigo and Kelly were clear about their calling to start an all-inclusive new faith community in this county. According to their website, when Kelly was asked about their vision, she said, "When we cast a net into the water, we don't get to pick and choose what kind of fish we catch. It's the same with the people we connect to within our community. We want to reach out to absolutely everybody, and our vision is to enable nations to experience transformation together."[1]

Gwinnett Country is a great location for a multiethnic, multiracial new church to flourish. The next logical question is, what sort of strategies for church planting would work well in this mission field? Rodrigo says, "We have two primary strategies in church planting in North Georgia—mother-daughter and parachute-drop strategies." These strategies are described earlier in chapter 8, but it's worth recalling that the parachute drop of classical missionary strategy is when a planter is sent into a territory to start a new faith community where the planter is not from that territory and there are no active partnerships with other churches or Christian institutions in the area. This is church planting from scratch.

Rodrigo spent time studying these two strategies in light of his vision to start a multiethnic church. After long hours of investigating which of these two strategies would have the greater potential to help him start and sustain an ethnically diverse church, he decided not to use either of these two models. Rodrigo explains,

> Parachute-drop is highly finance-driven strategy, and mother-daughter church is hard because most, if not all, existing churches within the area are homogeneous congregations.

It is fairly common not to adopt a single strategy when it comes to planting new churches or faith communities. Doing so is more like a puzzle, and the opportunities come in many different sizes and patterns. In a fast-changing mission field such as the United States, it makes a lot of sense to use a variety of strategies in starting new churches or faith communities in order to seize the opportunity for making a greater number of new, younger, and more diverse disciples of Jesus Christ. A one-hundred-piece-puzzle approach in this context would be proven inadequate because the context clearly calls for at least a 5,000-piece-puzzle strategy. In fact, a church planter should create her or his own church-planting strategy, one that will better serve the efforts of planting a distinctive type of new faith community in a unique location such as Gwinnett County. In the case of Rodrigo's vision of planting an ethnically diverse church, he knew that starting a multiethnic church is a complex enterprise. It offers opportunities and challenges in inviting and gathering people to become part of a new faith community around the vision of diversity and the collective experience of real transformation in the lives of people and the community as a whole. Rodrigo responded to this vision-inspired challenge by developing an implementation plan for the project. Given the situation, Rodrigo thought to himself,

> If I wanted to start a United Methodist brand of multiethnic, multiracial church, it [would be] better to develop a strategy that is anchored on the connectional system of The United Methodist Church.

He played with this idea for a while and then came up with a strategy that he referred to as the "Twelve Big Brothers Strategy in Church Planting"; this was how Rodrigo initially attempted to put together the pieces of his puzzle. He describes his plan in this way:

(A) Approach twelve United Methodist congregations and ask each one of them to support us in a very specific way. (B) Four [of these congregations will] support us with their presence, and that will include extending roughly five families each, so we could start with twenty families. (C) Each of these twelve congregations will contribute $12,000 a year for three years. (D) These partner-congregations will also support this project by one act of community and one act of evangelism service once a year. And (E) These churches will be praying for this new church start.

As Rodrigo learned, though, this approach looked good on paper, but it did not look so great in the real world. After diligently working with area churches and his annual conference, Rodrigo ended up with zero families and a one-time $2,500 in total contributions from two churches. This strategy, and therefore the project as a whole, was not working at that time. Rodrigo met with his district superintendent and a conference leader to discuss what needed to be done for this planting project. All of the parties decided to discontinue it. The strategy plan failed, but the vision was still clear, strong, and alive.

What happened next was the most interesting part of the story, and from it, we can learn some helpful principles and practices for starting a multiethnic, multiracial new faith community.

1. **A failed plan can be a set-up to create a new plan and gain momentum.**

    This is exactly what happened after Rodrigo's strategy plan did not produce the results he was expecting from it. Rodrigo recalls,

    I continued talking to people and kept casting the vision of organizing an ethnically diverse type of a church in a county that is richly diverse, yet every church in all the ZIP codes in Gwinnett country is homogeneous. Most people I met really liked the idea of being able to worship with people who look different from them.

Instead of allowing his failed plan to stop him from pursuing the vision that he received from God, Rodrigo and Kelly did not give in. Rather, they continued to believe in it and shared it with others. According to Rodrigo,

> A small group started gathering in our living room. Meanwhile, my district superintendent was looking for another appointment because he wanted me to move to another church appointment, but I requested to stay, and it was granted. By that time, our small group grew in numbers, and we outgrew our living room. In January 2016, our group decided to go to the high school nearby. Within three months, with sixty or more people committed to the vision, we launched The Nett Church in April 2016.

Currently, The Nett Church has three campuses that are thriving and living their common vision of a faith community that enables nations to experience transformation together in the name of Jesus.

2. **A new church can multiply even at the early stage of its growth and development as a new thing.**

In 2017, The Nett Church was a young, new faith community. They were in the midst of growing and strengthening their new church when they decided to take over an existing church nearby with twenty people in Sunday attendance. Rodrigo presented his idea to his district superintendent, who told him to do it by using the vital merger model. But as Rodrigo recalls,

> I didn't use that model. Instead, it ended up as a "hostile takeover." We killed their DNA and infused our DNA into the life of the church. It worked.

The community went from twenty people in 2017 to around 200 people in the summer of 2018 in this new location. Rodrigo and his coleaders used the same strategy in launching a second campus. They took over a church with roughly twenty to thirty people, which has grown to around one hundred people now and is still growing. In the summer of 2019, they employed the same approach in birthing their third campus. According to Rodrigo,

> We are actually doing things differently in this location. We are not launching worship at this time. Instead, we are repurposing the church facility to become a homeless shelter and an empowerment center to serve our community.

The Nett Church is a multiethnic, multiracial, and multiplying church. In slightly more than four years, The Nett Church started three healthy, diverse campuses that are still growing and making a difference in the lives of many people.

3. **Shifting from one model to another can be beneficial rather than a liability to the growth and sustainability of a new church plant.**

The Nett Church teaches and practices the principle that a new church can multiply from the beginning as long as it sticks to its vision and is led by an effective leadership team with strong buy-in and support from the people in the fellowship and the community. Also, the locations or facilities should be close to the heart and life of the people in the mission field. The Nett Church moved from a living room to a high school building. They then moved from that school gym to a church building (their first campus) and then replicated their church into two other church facilities. This is an amazing story that is still unfolding in a great way.

Even as The Nett Church shifted through different strategies and models for planting, they kept a common vision that drove their efforts and helped created a networked faith community in multiple contexts. This vision made the decision to multiply into multiple campuses pretty simple. Rodrigo recalls,

> We were in a high school. We had 120 people. According to our county, you cannot have a church building unless you have eight acres. So, without putting a shovel into the ground, we were going to need a million dollars. So, the idea of moving to a place, even if we just [renovate and improve it], we were going to end up in the upside

financially. It was just simply a business decision. And the second one was the fact that we have a church building on every corner in this county. So, it was this [question] of, how can we leverage our assets to advance our mission as a church?

Again, having a strong sense of mission for creating a multiethnic, multiracial faith community in a county that is ripe for these kinds of churches encouraged Rodrigo and his leadership team to replicate their DNA as a church in different facilities within Gwinnett County. Shifting models is okay, they feel, as long as doing so advances the vision and DNA of the church in each of these current locations or facilities of The Nett Church. In slightly more than three years, The Nett Church is fully financially sustainable with a yearly budget of more than $700,000.00 and with an investment of more than $1 million in their three campuses, free of debt.

4. **Intentionally integrating the value of prayer within the life and ministry of the church must be a practice of any church, whether new or existing.**

     Rodrigo puts a high value on prayer. He says,

     In planting these new faith communities in three locations, I believe I spent more time on my knees in prayer [than] I have done in my previous ten years as a pastor.

Every church planter will agree with Rodrigo that it is necessary to be intentional in prayer time with God. We don't know how a church planter could survive or operate expanding new churches without being intentional in prayer. Even Jesus himself knew that he needed to stay connected with God. He prayed, day and night, as an essential part of his daily routine and activities.

     There were moments during the creation of The Nett Church when Rodrigo wanted to quit pursuing his God-given vision. When he learned that he might be asked to return to serving a homogeneous congregation, he recalled thinking, *I'm going to be absolutely miserable, and I'm not going to be living into my calling.* In the beginning, with very few people in the church, no money, and nothing going very well, Rodrigo thought that this whole idea of starting a multiethnic and multiracial church was not going to lift off; it felt to him as though it were dead on arrival. During this time, Rodrigo admits feeling, "I lost home in my denomination and lost my confidence with my leadership."

However, his deep conviction that this was a call from God; the level of support and encouragement from his wife, children, and other people who were part of this project; and the level of intentionality in prayer by the whole church family truly made a big difference for Rodrigo as a leader and for The Nett Church as a new faith community. What we learn from their story is that when we quiet ourselves before God through prayer, we can have a more realistic approach to solving our problems. We can have the humility to accept failures as opportunities to mature in faith and in our leadership. We are able to welcome criticism with open minds and with a willingness to be better. And finally, we learn that our actions become an expression of the will of God, which is of the utmost importance.

5. **A church planter's family is an integral part of any church family, and its well-being is important for the welfare of the faith community.**

Rodrigo and other church planters know that the church's involvement and the well-being of their families and loved ones are very important parts of their ministry and should be treated with much care. Family vitally matters for Rodrigo, because it was with his family that he began hearing the call to plant a multiethnic, multiracial faith community. Rodrigo's family is a multiethnic family. He is Mexican American, and his wife, Kelly, is white. Three of their children are Mexican American, one is Chinese, and one is white. In Rodrigo's previous church, where he served as the pastor assigned to both the English-language service and the Spanish-language service, their family would come to worship at both services. After following this practice for a long time, the family recognized that they couldn't sustain this approach, so they decided to change their Sunday worship experience as a family. As Rodrigo recalls, "One Sunday we would attend the English-language service and then the next Sunday, the Spanish." After following this pattern for a while, one of their boys asked his parents, "Which service am I going to today—the English one or the Spanish?" It was during this time that Rodrigo realized he needed to take care of the spiritual needs of his family. He recalls,

> We were raising our children in a place where they had to pick and choose. There's just something fundamentally wrong with [that]. At that point, I made a decision that I wanted to be part of a church with my kids.

As mentioned earlier, Rodrigo's wife, Kelly, has been a strong partner-leader in birthing The Nett Church. According to Rodrigo,

> She provided the support to me that nobody can do better and more effectively than she does. She cares as much as I do. Her support in believing what we will and can do is just mind-blowing. Kelly is my number one critic but also my number one supporter. And she has really found a way to carry that balance.

The whole family is in this together, which is what really matters most.

It can be challenging, even overwhelming, to see 5,000 pieces of a puzzle spread out on a table and not know where to start putting them all together. Rodrigo Cruz and The Nett Church help show us that we can arrive at a plan to do it. We learn from their story that the location or target audience for any type of new faith community often includes an analysis of available resources, such as partner churches, denominational backing, prayer networks, financial support, facilities, and many more. Putting all these resources together and blending them with the gifts of the church planter, the support of his or her family, and the commitment of the whole faith community in pursuing a God-given vision all help in building a new church like The Nett Church.

In the next chapter, we will go deeper in exploring the question of "Where?" Where can we find the necessary resources, such as partners, money, and leaders, to name a few? Where is the best location? Where should we start a new church? Where is the next place to consider replicating your church's DNA?

10

Where to Plant?

[Jesus] called the twelve and began to send them out two by two, and gave them authority over the unclean spirits. He ordered them to take nothing for their journey except a staff; no bread, no bag, no money in their belts; but to wear sandals and not to put on two tunics. He said to them, "Wherever you enter a house, stay there until you leave the place. If any place will not welcome you and they refuse to hear you, as you leave, shake off the dust that is on your feet as a testimony against them." So they went out and proclaimed that all should repent. They cast out many demons, and anointed with oil many who were sick and cured them.

—MARK 6:7-13

Where should one start a new church? Often, this is the first question asked about new faith communities, and it is very tempting to pull out a map and some demographic overlays and just start dreaming. However, before beginning, it's essential to think through some priorities and evaluative criteria to help focus conversations and decisions about where to begin new faith communities. These three questions can guide determination of where to start a new church or new ministry:

1. Where is God leading the planter to start a new faith community?
2. Where are passionate leaders willing to put their lives into a new faith community?
3. Where are the people, partners, and resources needed to start a new faith community?

Although geography is important for a new faith community start, it turns out not to be predictive of the success of that new start. A good leader will succeed almost anywhere, but a bad leader likely won't succeed anywhere. More important, by far, is the spiritual vision of the new faith community planter, the commitment of the supporting partners, and the quality of the planting leaders. These three criteria and priorities are listed in order of importance, and no new church should be started unless it begins with a unanimous affirmation of God's calling to this endeavor by everyone involved.

Where Is God Calling the Planter?

The first step of any successful ministry is obedience to the call of God. In chapter 6, "How Are Churches Planted?" we discussed a process to discern a ministry strategy. The process of discerning a call to a specific people or location is roughly similar. Fortunately, God can be helpful in guiding a planter by offering up gifts, relationships, and history with a place or people-group. Perhaps the planter shares language or culture or life stage or occupation or education. Perhaps the planter has previous knowledge and relationships already established in a region. Perhaps the planter has always loved a city or spends every vacation getting to know a certain place. Curtis recalls having lunch with a potential planter and asking that person if they'd ever thought of starting a new church. The planter replied that they had, but only if it was in one particular city; it turned out that this was the same city where Curtis was looking for someone to plant a new church. This planter was thrilled to be invited to hear that as a calling from God. The planter's passions, capacity, and background can be helpful in narrowing down possible locations. Often, we can get some guidance from God by exploring how the Holy Spirit has been preparing a person to serve a particular community.

Faith communities and ministries are gatherings of people. As such, a planter is almost always focused on engaging with new people. Every person will engage new relationships in his or her own unique ways, and these ways will work more or less effectively with different kinds of people. Of course, planters can work with people outside their core affinity, but it's often easier and more fruitful to begin a new faith community among people with whom the planter has affinity. There are two kinds of affinity:

1.   There is affinity with people with whom the planter is attracted to minister.
2.   There is affinity with people who are attracted to minister with the planter.

Most people would prefer to surround themselves with people with whom they are attracted to minister. However, a more fruitful approach is to consider the people who are attracted to minister with the planter. Gathering people will occupy a lot of time and energy in a new faith community, and it will be easier to do if the planter is focused on groups of people who are already interested in knowing more about the planter.

Affinity, however, does have its limits. Reaching new people almost always requires communicating with people who are culturally different from the planter. Sometimes, these differences might be easily recognized through differences in language, accent, or clothing. More often, these differences will not be as noticeable. A helpful metaphor for talking about culture is that of an iceberg. For most icebergs, only about one-eighth of the total mass is visible above the waterline, with seven-eighths of the iceberg hidden from sight.[1] Culture is like that too, with most of it hidden from sight until you bump into it. One of the biggest challenges for most people starting a new ministry, new faith community, or new church is communicating with people who are not a part of "churched" culture. There is a specific set of language (hymn, praise, doxology), a specific set of practices (small group, potluck, bazaar), and a specific set of beliefs (discipleship, tithing, mission) shared by many people who already go to church in the United States. These generally aren't shared by the people who don't already go to a church. If the goal is to reach new people, the planter will need the capacity to communicate across this particular cultural divide, among others.

A planter's calling is not to "bring Christ" into a community. This kind of casual colonialism evokes the worst parts of Christian missionary history. Instead, a more helpful approach to church planting begins with the belief that God is already at work in the world, before and beyond the awareness of the established church and its missionaries or church planters. The first step in starting a new church is to trust God and, especially, to trust in God's Spirit that is moving in the world. For Methodists, this idea is connected to the Wesleyan description of God's prevenient grace. *Prevenient grace* is the work of God that enables and engages individual people both to recognize their need for God's love and to turn around to encounter and be embraced by God's justifying and saving grace. Like background radiation from the explosion of God's creating love, it still echoes through everything. The doctrine of prevenient grace is a part of the Wesleyan rejuvenation of reason and natural theology as a source of divine revelation that stands alongside the more Reformed emphasis on revelation through scripture alone. John Wesley, in his sermon *On Working Out Our Own Salvation*, describes this presence as God's light when he writes, "Everyone has some measure of that light, some faint glimmering ray, which, sooner or later, more or less, enlightens every [person] that cometh into the world."[2]

For new church planters, the idea that all people are already related to God's light means that their first task is not to introduce people to God but, instead, to help people find God already at work in their lives, their neighborhoods, and their communities. God's mission does not come as a new resident moving into the neighborhood. Rather, God is a longtime resident who is at least partially known to everyone. Church planting begins in trusting God's presence in the lives of the people and carefully listening to their stories to discern how to join with them in what God is already doing. Leonardo Boff articulates this incredibly well as he describes the inductive approach used by the Latin American liberation cell communities to start new churches:

> That reality is faith in the active presence of the risen
> One and of his Spirit at the heart of every human com-
> munity, efficaciously enabling it both to live the essential

values, without which there is no humanity, and to open out to the Absolute, without whom there is no dignity or salvation. This divine activity acquires a special density in the church. But it excludes no human person. This contemplative view modifies the manner of being church. Now the clergy moves into the midst of the people, toward persons already activated by the Spirit, which, before the arrival of the institutional church, was already shaping an anonymous church by its grace, its forgiveness. This is not a matter, then, of *transplanting* the church deductively, but of *implanting* the church inductively.[3]

Planters "find" church by following the florescent tracings of the Holy Spirit that have already preceded them into the mission field of the community. We use the term *planters* in this book, but this metaphor is helpfully limited by the fact that God has already planted the seed, and our efforts are focused on cultivation and harvest.

Where Do We Find Passionate Leaders?

A planter needs a team to start a new ministry, new faith community, or new church. The gathering of a team of coleaders who are willing to share and support the planter's vision is one of the most critical factors in bringing that vision to life. In reviewing new church plants for the past decade or so in The United Methodist Church, there has been a clear trend that those new churches that reached self-sufficiency and multiplying growth had developed a team of about a dozen leaders before launching weekly public worship. There is nothing magical about the number twelve. It has great symbolism for the Bible (the twelve tribes of Israel, the twelve disciples), and it has great usefulness for group dynamics (two discussion groups of six, four working teams of three). Twelve is big enough that it feels like a good-sized team, but it is small enough that it can be led by one leader. It's a good number, but it's not a guarantee. Some new churches have started with teams that are smaller (but not too much smaller), while some have launched with much larger teams.

Often, when a new ministry is starting, planters will want to involve as many new people as possible, as quickly as possible. On its core leadership team, however, a new church plant is also going to want the right people. In general, plants should be looking for people who have these characteristics:

- **Growing spiritually:** Leaders should model the discipleship journey that is at the heart of their ministry.
- **Highly relational:** Leaders have to relate to others, whether they are extroverted or introverted.
- **Passionately invested:** Leaders need to be excited about what they are doing together, and they need to display that passion through their investments of time and money.
- **On the planter's team:** Leaders need to believe in their team leader. They are people who will support the planter's vision, strategy, and mission. Critics and outside advice can be helpful but not in this core team.

In addition to these general characteristics, a leadership team will be greatly benefited by having one or more people with these specific skills or gifts:

- **Spiritual maturity:** Someone, besides the planter, who can mentor and model a deep faith.
- **Finance:** Someone who is good with numbers and isn't afraid to talk finances.
- **Organization:** Someone who can keep track of details, calendars, and information.
- **Leadership:** Someone, besides the planter, who can model leadership and strategy.
- **Prayer:** Someone who can constantly remind the team to pray and who is always praying for the leadership-team members.
- **Hospitality:** Someone who knows how to throw a great party and will teach their secrets to the entire team.
- **Assistance:** Someone who will be able to step into any role or task and offer assistance if needed.

Where do new planters find these people? Quite simply, planters have to start by meeting a lot of new people, understanding their spiritual journey, inviting them into discipleship through the new ministry, and then mentoring them as they develop into leaders. This takes intention, planning, and focus, but it begins with meeting a lot of people.

Meeting a Lot of People

Every new ministry, church, or faith community is made up of people, and lots of them. Planters need to meet hundreds of people throughout their communities and neighborhoods. Most of these people will not just show up at a Bible study or worship service. Instead, in order to build a strong enough relationship so that new people might be willing to accept an invitation to discipleship, someone will have to go where these new people are already gathering, get invited to parties that they are already throwing, and be welcomed around tables where they are already seated. Some people who start new ministries or communities are very extroverted; some are quite introverted. Regardless of their personality, all successful planters learn to be great at meeting new people.

Meeting new people is a social skill that can be learned and practiced. It's not inborn or a permanent facet of personality. Although extroverted people enjoy it more, introverted people can do it well and find enjoyment in it also. Different cultures have different patterns and expectations about how formal or informal relationships are established. Planters need to be aware of their own personality and strengths, as well as the social patterns of the people they are trying to reach. For decades, one of the best resources on how to learn to network with new people has been Dale Carnegie. In his 1936 primer *How to Win Friends and Influence People*, Carnegie provides these principles for meeting new people:[4]

1. **Become genuinely interested in and curious about other people.**
   Ask them observational questions about themselves. Inquire about their families, jobs, hobbies, and interests.

2. **Smile.**
   Being positive is attractive to others. This isn't about being inauthentic but about nurturing what is encouraging in yourself and in others through conversation.

3. **Remember that a person's name is to that person the sweetest and most important sound in any language.**
    Use the person's name back to them. Try to repeat it aloud a few times during the conversation to help you remember it and use it when you meet again.

4. **Be a good listener. Encourage others to talk about themselves.**
    Most conversation is listening, not talking. Pay attention to the other person. Take mental note of what the person is saying and how he or she is saying it. Ask relevant follow-up questions and draw connections and interrelationships where you see commonality.

5. **Talk in terms of the other person's interests.**
    In casual encounters, people are mostly motivated by their own self-interest. Seek to understand the other person and his or her hopes and expectations. Do not try to get the other person to understand you but allow him or her to shape the conversation.

6. **Make the other person feel important and do it sincerely.**
    Everyone has some level of expertise or experience from which others could sincerely benefit. Seek what makes the other person great to know and thank him or her for sharing that.

A key to building new relationships with new people is learning to listen. Listening is countercultural in the mass media of the United States. Taking time to stop, pay attention, and listen to another person can be a profound and unique offering of grace and hospitality. Curtis worked with a planter who began networking for his new faith community by meeting people and introducing himself as "The Minister of Listening." By beginning in a posture of learning, he was better able to build trust and initiate relationships. How does someone listen well? Again, this is a skill that can be practiced and learned. Good listening requires one to do the following:

Focus

♡ Make meaningful eye contact but do not stare. Look at the person's eyes, mouth, hands, and posture as the person is communicating.

- ☞ Provide appropriate nonverbal feedback, such as smiling, laughing, inclining your head, and nodding.
- ☞ Dismiss distractions by focusing your attention on the person who is speaking. Ignore other conversations, your internal monologue, and your phone.

Understand

- ☞ During the conversation, ask relevant questions that add to your understanding of what the person is saying or feeling. Don't interrogate the person but probe as deeply as the individual seems comfortable.
- ☞ Interpret emotional clues from the person to whom you're listening. This includes tone of voice, expression, posture, hand motions, and pace of speaking. Most information in a conversation is communicated through nonverbal clues. These clues vary from culture to culture, so pay attention to cultural differences and ask for clarity when you misunderstand.
- ☞ If appropriate, you can summarize back to the person something you have just heard to make sure you understand it fully. Try it by saying, "I think that I heard you say . . ."

Nurture

- ☞ Listening to someone else's story is an honor. Respect the other person and what that person is saying. Practice appropriate confidentiality and experience all listening with gratitude.
- ☞ Encourage the other person to share as much as he or she is comfortable with, but don't push beyond that level. Listening well should invite further conversations that may go deeper. Your goal is to begin a relationship, so nurture further conversations.
- ☞ Share from your own experiences but only if asked to do so and only if appropriate. Listening can be a powerful practice in and of itself, so don't feel pressure to provide deep advice, correction, or opinion. Your presence as a listener is probably enough.

The Evangelism Question

As Christians practice building positive relationships with other people, eventually they will be asked about their motivations. Because Christians live according to the teachings of Jesus, their lives and relationships should have a different quality that is obvious when people get to know them. Christians should be demonstrably more generous, more inclusive, more caring, more hopeful, more patient, and more gracious. People whom Christians meet will be confused by this difference, and it should cause them to ask questions. This is "The Evangelism Question," and it usually takes the form of an inquiry into why the Christian is behaving in such an unexpected way. Sometimes, it's asked in curiosity; sometimes, it's asked in suspicion, and samples of The Evangelism Question include the following:

- "Why are you being so nice to me?"
- "You're not like other people. Why is that?"
- "Why are you so weird?"
- "So, what do you really want? You must want something."
- "I don't understand why anyone would act that way; why do *you*?"

When Christians have given witness to God's love through their relationships, they should also be prepared to answer questions about their witness through testimony. This testimony should describe their personal motivations, but it shouldn't be transactional or manipulative. An authentic response might be, "I'm kind to other people because in my church, we believe in a kind God who commands us to be kind to others." In contrast, a transactional response might be, "I'm kind to others so that they'll come to my church." Every response to The Evangelism Question is designed to continue a conversation and deepen a relationship. An invitation to church or Christian discipleship is likely to be received only when it's offered within the halo of authentic care and concern for the other person. And it's likely to require multiple cycles of questions, responses, and invitations before someone takes the next step in the faith journey. Sometimes the best fruit of a conversation is the promise of another conversation.

How can a Christian prepare to respond to The Evangelism Question? It takes some forethought and practice. Sometimes developing an "elevator speech" can be helpful for planters. This is a common phrase used in marketing training to describe the brief collection of phrases and ideas that encapsulate and interest a listener in a salesperson's project or product. This brief message should take only as long to share as a quick elevator ride—so, a minute or two, at most. Although called a "speech," it isn't delivered as if the person is on a stage or behind a pulpit. Because it is a collection of prearranged phrases and ideas, it is composed and articulated in different ways, depending upon the person and the context. A planter might say something different to a potential fundraising donor who already goes to an established church than the manner in which he or she does to a new neighbor met while walking the dog.

It is hard to think up an elevator speech and improvise in the moment; most people will need to prepare their thoughts ahead of time and practice a lot. Often, people take too long to describe what they are doing because they haven't thought it through ahead of time. This can make a planter sound insecure and uncommitted to the new ministry or faith community. A good vision and mission statement will help provide inspiring ideas and useful phrases; but ultimately, the most important thing to convey is personal authenticity and passion: Why does this matter to you as an individual? Why are you excited about this? What is so great that you have to share it with your new friend? Why does this invitation matter? How has involvement in this ministry or faith changed your life, and how could it change your friend's life?

Building a Relationship System

Leaders almost always emerge from within an established network of relationships. Key to successfully building a system of relationships for any new ministry, new church, or new faith community will be understanding how people are connected to the planter, other leaders, and the new project. Just because a planter has someone's contact information doesn't mean that person is a core part of the planter's leadership team; that frequently takes a journey of deepening relationship and connection. Sometimes, this journey can be helpfully understood in terms of different orbits. Imagine that a new church is a planet with gravity that attracts people into closer and closer orbit. The closer a person is to the ministry, the more he or she is affected by its gravity and influence. Part of helping build a community is thinking through the different orbits and determining how to help people draw into a closer orbit. In many growing ministries, churches, and faith communities, there will be relative engagement-orbits for people that correspond to categories similar to these:

1. Core
- people who are committed coleaders in leadership or on a launch team
- people who practice growing in personal discipleship and who coach others
- people who regularly invite others into community

2. Committed
- committed participants who come to most early events
- people who are growing in discipleship
- people who occasionally provide leadership or invite other new people into community

3. Participants
- people who have a personal relationship with the planter or with a core team member
- people who participate in some early events
- people interested in growing in discipleship but who might not have begun
- people who might have brought a friend along to an event or activity

4. Interested
- people who have been invited but haven't yet participated in a community event or activity
- people who have expressed interest in your new ministry, church, or faith community
- people who might have a personal relationship with the planter or a team member

5. Prospects

- people from whom the planter has received contact information but with whom the planter hasn't yet had conversation or determined their interest level
- people who might be referrals from other people

Once a new ministry project has been defined and its different levels of engagement or orbits have been determined, then a plan is needed for tracking communication with people in each orbit. Without a system, new ministries are likely to lose contact with people as the ministry grows and a greater number of new people enter the picture. At its most basic, this system can simply be a notebook with the name and contact information of each person and an indication of his or her involvement. For communication-tracking purposes, it's helpful to group people into their obits and then transfer their information into a new orbit section when they draw closer. Keeping a digital file makes it even easier. By organizing people into a document, their information can simply be copied and pasted as they change orbits. A simple spreadsheet or database might be more complex, but it allows contact information to be more easily imported into social media, email, or postal communication systems. Planters can also use software such as constituent relationship management (CRM) or church management software (CMS). In addition to managing the contact information and orbits, many of these can be programmed to set reminders that automate contacting people at regular intervals, based on their level of involvement.

With people's information in their different orbits, the next step is to build a system to contact them following a regular pattern. *Core* and *Committed* people might be contacted each week, with a face-to-face meeting set for at least monthly. *Prospects* might be contacted at least monthly and offered personal invitations to meet with the planter. Each level of the different obits should be carefully thought through, asking these questions:

- [I should] contact [this person] how often?
- Contact for which discipleship activities?
- Contact for which invitation activities?
- Contact for which fundraising activities?
- Contact for which other reasons?

Once these decisions have been made, then a planter can develop the system to ensure that these contacts are made both consistently and well. Building and following a system will make the task of meeting a lot of new people easier to manage and will enable the leaders to continue to put the focus on meeting new people, even as the ministry grows.

How Many People Are "A Lot"?

If a new church or ministry is planning to have a dozen committed coleaders as part of its launch team in the first year, how many contacts will it need to make each day? Curtis and Bener asked several successful planters and denominational leaders how many people would need to be contacted to find twelve leaders. Their responses varied; but in general, their experience was that many new starts will use as their guide something like the following ratios of involvement (although, these may need to be adjusted up or down, based on the religious receptivity of the people the new church is trying to reach):

- 12: *Core* coleaders who are growing in discipleship and inviting others
- 36: *Committed* participants in most early activities (3x Core)
- 72: Occasional *participants* in some early activities (2x Committed)
- 214: *Interested* people whom you've met (3x Participants)
- 428: *Prospects* who give you their contact information (2x Interested)
- 1,284: Number of new people to meet this year (3x Prospects)
- 25: Weekly contacts (over 52 weeks)

As they come on board, additional core leaders will also help with contacts, so filling out all these categories won't fall exclusively upon one person. Each contact should always be asked whether that person knows someone else who could be contacted, as a lot of good contacts will emerge from referrals. Given how important gathering a leadership team is to the success of a new ministry, the initial focus should be on finding core coleaders, not necessarily on having large crowd events (unless these events are part of the key strategy for finding leaders).

"The Granola Rule"

Almost every new ministry, new faith community, new congregation, or new church will have an experience with "The Granola Rule." Though it may seem a bit harsh, good leaders will help steer volunteers away from destructive behavior in a loving and gracious way. A new ministry will inevitably attract some dysfunctional and destructive people who will want to exercise their dysfunctions and destructions within the leadership team of the new thing. We call it "The Granola Rule" because it's the rule that all new things will attract more than their fair share of "flakes and nuts." At the beginning of a new ministry, planters will be eager to enlist the help of anyone who seems interested. They need people to get things started. Most of these people will be great, but some of them will see this as an opportunity to attempt to behave in ways other groups or congregations have not tolerated. Because these people are new and are relatively unknown, they may test the boundaries of acceptable behavior within the new ministry's team. Their misbehavior can taint the emerging team and drive more emotionally mature people out. Planters will need to be careful and constantly reinforce the limits of acceptable behavior within the team.

A particular problem within emerging church groups is people looking to grab power and control of the group to further their own agenda. They may have strong beliefs about a particular church program, a piece of theology, or the color of the carpet. Sometimes, these beliefs may even be appropriate, but if there are any people who seek to usurp others' leadership in favor of their own, then they have stepped over the line. Planters will do well not to let them or their pet peeve drive the vision or mission of the leadership group. Instead, leadership should be focused on the vision and mission. If there are some who are not willing to join in that vision and mission, then they should be asked to find a different group, ministry, or church that is a better fit for their passion.

Bullying is another common behavior in church groups, and it's particularly common among people who have had a lot of previous church experience. In many churches, physical and emotional bullying is tacitly accepted, and bullies have become used to getting their way through threats, manipulation, and intimidation. Some common expressions include the following:

∅ "Well, if we don't get what we want, we'll just leave the church."
∅ "I hear everybody's complaining about this, so, you'd better do something."
∅ "If you want our financial offering, you'd better do it this way."

Bullying through physical, emotional, or financial manipulation has no place in any group, ministry, congregation, community, or church. Leaders will need to set a positive example of acceptable behavior and clearly call out bullying behavior in order to describe its inappropriateness.

Where Can We Find the Necessary People, Resources, and Partners?

Finally, the last consideration in thinking about where to start a new church or new faith community is the availability of people, resources, and partners. Too often, planning a new ministry begins with this question, but it should be secondary to the discernment of the planter and the passion of a leadership team. As we mentioned earlier, good leaders will often find ways to succeed in almost every situation, but poor leaders will always fail everywhere. Too often, the desire to start a new church doesn't start with a clear calling or identification of a leader but, instead, begins with the identification of growth in a target population or with the availability of an empty church facility; this is putting the cart before the horse. Just because the population of an area is growing and prosperous doesn't mean that the churches in that area will grow. And there are thousands of growing churches located in declining communities. The engine of growth in any new project is always the leadership, not the demographics or resources available to those leaders.

People

New ministries, faith communities, and churches should begin where people are living. Demographic information is readily available in many forms, but the data is only as good as its interpretation. It's easy to get overwhelmed and inundated by charts and tables and graphs showing detailed descriptions of the number and kinds of people living in an area.

This information is helpful in forming general hypotheses, but it often needs fleshing out in order to be helpful in planning a new ministry.

The first step in interpreting demographic data is to drill down into it in order to understand lifestyle segmentation within the population being studied. Secular marketing companies have collected a tremendous amount of information on the behaviors of people, and from this they have further segmented groups into lifestyle segments. These segments are often more predictive of behavior than basic demographic information about income, ethnicity, age, or gender. Many demographic services will provide a breakdown of these segments, and some church-specific services (such as *missioninsite.com*) will even provide research on religious-life preferences, including preferred kinds of worship experiences, pastoral leadership style, and financial giving patterns.

The second step in interpreting demographics is to walk or drive around an area and observe how demographic trends are actually playing out in that specific community. Pay attention to signs and notices: What languages are they in, and what concerns are being shared? Pay attention to which businesses are opening and thriving and which ones are deteriorating and closing. Pay attention to which homes are available for sale or rent and how long they've been on the market. Stop in public places and observe who is there and what they are doing. Read a local newspaper or study local community groups online. All of this will help incarnate abstract data into the real lives of real people.

The final step in demographic research is to test your theories and hypotheses by talking to people. Go to some places where locals go and ask a few questions. Tell them that you're considering moving into the area and want information about the community. Contact people you may know—or people who may know someone you know—and speak to them. Contact community leaders and set up an appointment to have a conversation with them about the needs and resources of the community. All of this is to help develop as specific a view of the people as possible.

Resources

Most new ministries, faith communities, and churches will need outside funding support to get started. The biggest expenses are usually staff payroll and facility rental or purchase. When planning something new, it's a good idea to scale the financial cost to fit the capacity of the people who will become a part of the new ministry. In the United States, we've seen a recent wave of very expensive, worship-first, highly-attractive, and spectacularly produced new churches launch and do pretty well at drawing a crowd of young adults. Sadly, though, these churches were too expensive to be financially supported by the heavily indebted young adults in their congregation, and they have run out of money and closed within the first year or two after launching.

New starts will find startup money from individual donors, denominations, and sponsoring congregations. Like most venture capitalists and philanthropists, these outside funders will expect to see specific benchmarks of growth and, eventually, the ministry to become financially self-sustaining. For this reason, scale matters. Financial expenses should match the potential financial income within the community. Expenses can be reduced through lowering payroll by using bivocational or volunteer staff, using low-cost facilities such as existing church buildings at off-times, and relying upon the lower-cost marketing and promotion strategies of personal invitation and individual conversations.

When long-term financial capacity is built into the launch strategy, it will keep the new start from running out of money too early. Like demographics, available launch funding does not determine the success of a new church. Plenty of well-funded ministries have failed, while many underfunded ministries have succeeded. That said, financial constrictions are a major reason why otherwise healthy ministries have been discontinued.

Where a new ministry or faith community gathers makes a difference in who feels comfortable participating. For this reason, facility selection should grow out of the mission, vision, and calling of the new ministry. Too often, facility selection precedes any other concern and constrains the ministry instead of enhancing it. It may make perfect sense to a group of established church leaders that their comfortable and available sanctuary should be used to start a new church within a church for a group of nearby college students; however, those young people may see that same sanctuary as a barrier to inviting their friends who have sworn never to set foot in a church. Facilities should be selected based on three criteria:

1. **Comfort of the participants.** Is this a place where the people who will potentially participate feel comfortable? Is it a place where they already go, like a school (for young families) or a bar (for younger adults)? Will it evoke the atmosphere desired for the kind of gathering held, such as *inspiring* for worship or *friendly* for fellowship?

2. **Visibility.** Is this place widely known, easily recognized, and quickly found by the potential participants? A known location gives assurance and familiarity to new people and serves as a constant reminder of the faith community that gathers in that space, even if they rent it only occasionally.

3. **Affordability and availability.** Is the facility financially affordable, and is it available when and how the new faith community wants it? Does it have sufficient space at that time for the planned number of people without being too large or too crowded? Is there sufficient parking, and is traffic manageable at the time when it is planned to be used? Are there extra fees for overtime staff or cleaning?

When these three criteria are applied, they will often cause planters to think more creatively about what spaces and facilities are strategically more helpful. It can often lead to unexpected and innovative locations that are more interesting to people who are not already going to church.

Partners

New churches, faith communities, and ministries are part of the interconnected web of the apostolic and universal church of Christ. As such, they rarely stand completely alone, but, instead, they are supported by partner churches from their denominations, networks, or communities. A new faith community partner is any church, congregation, or organization that supports the launch of a new faith community with one or more of these four areas of support:

1. **Spiritual support**. New faith communities need extensive prayer and encouragement. A partner church commits to offering spiritual support through regular prayer for the new faith

community and its leaders—for example, by sending cards of encouragement or by offering letters of support.

2. **Material support.** New faith communities need stuff. A partner church commits to providing some of the physical items the new faith community may need to get started. This might include hosting a housewarming party or a baby shower for the new faith community and help by providing things such as portable nursery equipment, coffeepots, chairs, sound/video gear, signage, Bibles, or other useful items.

3. **Leadership support.** New faith communities need leaders. A partner congregation or organization might lend some leaders to the new faith community as short-term missionaries who could help with specific launch tasks (such as phone calls, distributing door-hangers, greeting, children's ministry workers, or financial management) or who might commit to helping through the first year or two of the launch. Some might even choose to stay with the new faith community. These leaders should be blessed and prayed over by the partner congregation before being sent out, and their home church should keep in contact with them to take full advantage of the exciting things they are learning as they journey with the new faith community.

4. **Financial support.** New faith communities need money. A partner congregation or organization might want to help provide some of the financial support for the new faith community. This can be in the form of a one-time gift or ongoing contributions.

A partner church receives a lot of benefit from its investment and relationship with a new church or new ministry. New faith communities are the research-and-development arm of the church, where they intentionally experiment with new ways of being church that creatively adapt to meet the changing dynamics of a mission field.

Partnering with a new faith community gives an established church direct access to what is being learned within the new faith community. New faith communities operate at a different pace than established organizations or congregations. Because they are new, they make decisions and changes more quickly. Partnering with a new faith community can help pick up the pace of change within a partnering organization as it participates in and is affected by a more rapid ministry partner. The change of pace can help the partnered group more quickly implement adaptive changes to engage its own mission field.

New faith communities are constantly raising and training new leaders. A great way to learn about leadership development is to have leaders of existing churches volunteer within a new faith community's ministry. They will experience firsthand a new pattern of raising and training new leaders.

New faith communities focus on contextualized evangelism within their mission field. Because they are constantly reaching new people, new faith communities often have an excellent understanding of what is actually connecting with people within their mission field. A partner congregation or organization can learn from their accumulated experiences and practices.

And, finally, new faith communities are a blessing. As new faith communities bless their participants and communities with life-altering, world-changing ministry, they give their partners the chance to be a part of sharing God's blessings with others. This shared blessing is the gift of God to the church and to the community where the new faith community is planted. In the next chapter, we will explore how to discern the timing of when to plant a new faith community.

11

Where Leads to When

Jesus went about all the cities and villages, teaching in their synagogues, and proclaiming the good news of the kingdom, and curing every disease and every sickness. When he saw the crowds, he had compassion for them, because they were harassed and helpless, like sheep without a shepherd. Then he said to his disciples, "The harvest is plentiful, but the laborers are few; therefore ask the Lord of the harvest to send out laborers into his harvest."

—MATTHEW 9:35-38

How do you know when it's the right time to change a church-planting model? For example, when do you move from a church within a church model to a semiautonomous, stand-alone campus? How do you know when it's the right time to cut ties with an anchor church and start a new campus? How have you and your coleaders made those decisions? How have you known it's the right time to make a substantial change like that? These are common questions always asked by church planters whenever they have to make a change or transition, whether it is a change of model, a change of location, or both. It boils down to this question: When should we start something new?

Definitely, timing is a critical element for consideration when it comes to making a big move that will change the overall situation of a new church start. Although timing is a critical piece in decision making, there are other interplaying pieces or factors that are also part of the big picture, which are also equally critical elements. Having an appropriate strategy, a clear alignment with the vision of the church, a high level of buy-in from key leaders and other stakeholders are some of those factors—just to name a few—that require serious consideration by the leadership team of a new church. If the desired change or transition that will have a lasting impact on the life and mission of the new church is to come to fruition, then timing and other factors have to be dealt with at a high level of importance by the church leadership. Thus, the church's response to the question, "When should we start something new?" should never be taken lightly but with much care, lots of prayer, and honest conversations between the lead planter and the church-planting team. With a firm strategy, with everyone fully on board, and with a clear sense of the Holy Spirit's guidance, almost any time is the right time to start something new.

Now, you may be thinking to yourself, *That kind of claim is easier said than done*, right? If so, then you are absolutely correct. Yet, it can be done. It is risky, but it is worth it, if the goal is to invite new people into new faith communities that help them transform into new disciples of Jesus Christ and get them involved in making a difference in the lives of people and communities.

Planter Story: Aaron Saenz and Valley Praise United Methodist Church

Valley Praise United Methodist Church has campuses in Harlingen and Santa Rosa, as well as a new, third campus launching in McAllen, Texas. All three communities are in the region of South Texas known locally as The Valley. Aaron Saenz, the lead pastor of Valley Praise, shared with us some of his valuable insights and practical steps for how to determine the right time and also what goes into making those determinations or decisions to start something new. There are several lessons we can learn from

the story of Valley Praise about how they have made major decisions in
making changes or transitions over the course of the life of this church.

1. **It is time to make a shift when your church is clear about
   its purpose and ready to live with it wholeheartedly.**

   Valley Praise was initially started in February 2006 by Rev.
   Janne Clinton in a cafetorium of Gutierrez Middle School in
   Harlingen, Texas. Reverend Clinton served this new faith community for the very short period of five months, until she retired
   in July 2006.

   Her retirement paved the way for Pastor Aaron Saenz to
   serve as the lead pastor of an offsite worship service of the First
   United Methodist Church in Harlingen. By that time, this new
   church of around forty people was essentially a restart, while
   keeping the relationship with First Church. Aaron recalls that
   most of those forty people wanted more of a contemporary feeling and style of worship. So, Aaron made the first major change
   at Valley Praise, which happened quickly. The church went from
   almost exclusively providing a worship style catered to the people
   who were already involved in the church to an intentional community engagement by reaching out and building relationships
   with people in the community. Worship became more than just
   a style; it became a strategy for engaging people with the gospel
   of Jesus Christ. Worship and community events were heavily
   emphasized throughout the first four years of Valley Praise under
   Aaron's leadership. And they grew from having forty people in
   June 2006 to an average of 200 in worship attendance in 2010.

   When they hit this mark of growth and felt confident with
   the vitality of the church, they made another major shift: With
   the shared discernment and support of First United Methodist
   Church, they moved from a mother-daughter church model to a
   standalone church model. Both groups determined that it was
   the right time for First United Methodist Church to release
   Valley Praise to become a standalone new church start. Aaron
   recalls,

   > It was for the sake of the growth, health, and bright
   > future of Valley Praise that First United Methodist

Church of Harlingen released Valley Praise to be a new church plant.

2. **It is time to make a shift if it will help your church be in a better position to build connections and strengthen relationships with the people in your community.**

Moving forward with the decision to become a standalone new church, Valley Praise faced major setbacks along the way. After they did a public launch at a new location in 2010, about seventy people went back to the mother church. With fewer people in the church and not enough money in their bank account, Valley Praise, in essence, went back to the drawing board to re-strategize. Aaron relied upon his unique gifts in a way that would help move Valley Praise forward in ministry. He says,

> I'm from the Valley. I'm a Valley boy, and so for me, in this culture, it's important to have somebody who speaks the language. And when I say "language," it is beyond [my] being bilingual. It is more of a cultural language here in the Valley.

Most of the communities in the Valley have substantial Hispanic populations, including Harlingen, McAllen, and Brownsville. The Valley is mostly now populated with third, fourth, and fifth generations of Mexican Americans and Latinx. The Valley is generally bilingual and has its own culture or way of living. Aaron describes his ministry this way:

> My cultural understanding of the Valley enabled me to know what it is that people are looking for because [they're] the very things that I need and I'm looking for, for myself and my family. And to know the things that are necessary for life here and be able to inform and integrate those cultural values, customs, and practices into the life and ministry of Valley Praise and use them well in building relationships with people in the community greatly helped the church to overcome the challenges and sustain its strength and vitality as a new church.

A strong affinity with the culture of the people in the Valley and intentional efforts of reflecting the "Valley culture" helped Valley Praise Church to better connect with people in these communities. Valley Praise was able to reach their goal of becoming a chartered and autonomous congregation in 2012. Thus, the move to become a standalone faith community brought the church closer to the people in the Valley and made them stronger as a new faith community.

3. **When God shows your church an opportunity to go to new locations to expand your mission and ministry, it is time to make a move.**

With all the major changes that they experienced over the first eight years of Valley Praise—a shift in leadership from Pastor Clinton to Pastor Saenz, a shift from a mother-daughter church model to a standalone new church start, a shift from focusing on worship style to intentional community engagement and worship as a strategy for connecting people with the gospel, and a shift from meeting at a middle school to having their own place—Valley Praise Church knows very well when it's the right time to start something new. And they also know very well that every decision they made was not free from troubles and setbacks. The church knew about these challenges and learned how to handle each one of them by the grace and guidance of the Holy Spirit as they moved forward.

In 2014, two years after Valley Praise became a chartered United Methodist congregation, the church bought the Sears Service Center in Harlingen, Texas, which is now identified as the Broadcast Campus of the church. Aaron recalls,

> This building used to be a place where they repair lawn mowers, washers, dryers, and other stuff. We flipped it, and we've been here since 2014.

Today, it is place of worship and a facility where people gather and grow as disciples of Jesus Christ. Valley Praise continues to grow and gain momentum in making a difference in the lives of people in Harlingen.

In 2017, an opportunity to expand the reach of their mission and ministry became very clear in Santa Rosa, Texas, which is about ten miles away from their original campus. In this small town of 3,000 people, Valley Praise took over an existing United Methodist congregation with only eight remaining faithful members of the church. In three years' time at this campus, they grew this second campus from eight people to a one hundred-person worshiping congregation. Aaron says, "The Santa Rosa community considers our church their community's church."

Not too long after launching a successful ministry in Santa Rosa, in 2020, God opened up another opportunity for expansion for Valley Praise, in another location about thirty-five miles away from the original campus. After praying about this new opportunity for growth, Valley Praise decided to send one of their pastors to launch a campus in McAllen, Texas. Pastor Kevin, along with his wife and their two boys, moved to McAllen to start another Valley Praise campus in this new location. In McAllen, there was a United Methodist church building that had closed more than six years earlier. The goal was to go into this community, use that church facility as their mission outpost, and start building relationships with the people in this neighborhood, just as they had done in Santa Rosa. And, says Aaron, perhaps understatedly, "It's been a good ride."

Remember, it is time to make a move when God clears the way for an opportunity to expand your church's mission in a new location.

We asked Aaron, "Are there other lessons that you want other church planters to learn from your journey as a lead pastor of Valley Praise Church?" He quickly responded by saying,

> In my opinion, it's just necessary to make big changes every once in a while for the sake of making changes, so people don't get too comfortable. I'm a believer in that.

We found Aaron's response to be very honest, inspiring, and scary at the same time. Let's refresh our memory a bit about the timeline and what has actually happened during these years in the life and ministry of Valley Praise Church. We could track that every two years following their chartering as a new church, in 2012 through 2020, they made major moves, including taking over two campuses, flipping church buildings, funding campaigns, starting and growing worship services in multiple locations, engaging communities, equipping leaders and making disciples of new believers of Jesus Christ, and everything else that goes on in between with all of these major tasks. There is a rhythm of starting something new at Valley Praise. Aaron recalls,

> We made big moves in 2010, 2012, 2014, 2016, 2018, and 2020. So, it's almost like it takes a year to build something, to launch something. Then, you take a year to recover; and then, you go right back at it again.

This is what we meant when we said it is both exciting and scary at the same time. And for other church planters who want to learn more from the example of the ministry at Valley Praise Church, Pastor Aaron Saenz offers the following tips.

1. **Develop a discipline or rhythm of starting something new and make it a part of your church's DNA.**

    Aaron frequently poses the following question to his leadership team and to the whole congregation: "What's our next big thing in the next two years?" Every person in the church knows that within the span of two years, there is going to be another new thing that God will ask and empower them to do to further strengthen their ongoing ministries across their current campuses and to expand their ministry and mission with more new people in new locations. Aaron describes this kind of mindset:

    > It's kind of like you climb to that next plateau, you sit there, and you enjoy the view for a year; and then next year, you climb again, and then you enjoy the view for a year. Since 2010, we've been running like that. And there's something about an expectation of change and an expectation of newness that if you don't do that, people are like, "Whoa, what's going on? Are we dying?" So, that's part of it.

2. **Develop an intentional approach for preparing, empower-
    ing, and mobilizing the whole church to start something
    new.**

    Valley Praise would not have been as successful if they had
    not set up an approach that helped each person in the church be
    fully equipped to pitch in and get excited to make each of these
    major moves. According to Aaron,

    > I'm really big on the Spirit of God moving, number one,
    > and then the Spirit of God moves *us*, which means we
    > need to continue to elevate that temperature. And when
    > I say "elevate the temperature," I mean getting people
    > excited, getting people oriented around and focused on
    > our next big move. We haven't done any of these without
    > being prepared, equipped, and excited to move forward.

    The ingredients for a fruitful ministry, as we have seen with
    Valley Praise Church, include clear expectations, accompanied
    by a deliberate approach to prepare and equip church people
    to work together so that they can rally and mobilize the whole
    church with the excitement needed to do something really great
    for God and the people in their community.

3. **Develop a churchwide practice of deep listening with
    one another and, most especially, listening with God and
    discerning God's directions before taking the next steps.**

    Pastor Saenz and his church know when to act to start some-
    thing new and when to take a pause for more reflection. Taking
    a pause or postponing your next action steps doesn't mean your
    church is losing its focus, weakening its commitment for mission,
    or is in trouble or struggling. In contrast, it is a special moment for
    the Spirit of God to allow the church to listen with one another
    and to seek God's guidance and directions. In the case of Valley
    Praise opening up their third campus, in McAllen, the expecta-
    tion was set, and the whole church was excited. And yet, they
    decided to postpone the launch of it for one year because they
    discerned at that time that they were not ready. Aaron recalls,

When we do make the move, there may be some who don't agree with it or who are not comfortable. It's okay. We bring them along in conversations. So, even if some didn't agree or were not too excited about the project, everybody feels like they've been heard. And usually, they'll say, "Let's see what happens."

Setting the expectation and getting the church ready and prepared to move forward are things that need to happen as part of the mobilization of the whole church to start something new.

4. **Develop a deep desire for learning and maturing yourself as you lead your church in learning and maturing as well.** You lead your church in this aspect of learning and maturing by your example. There are certain stages of development for your new church where you may feel as though you have hit a wall or come to the end of the road and are stuck. When Aaron started making a move from Valley Praise being a single, standalone church to becoming a multisite church, he realized that he was ill-equipped to lead this type of work; he needed help. So, he went outside of his comfort zone to find help, and he eventually found it. Aaron recalls,

> If I need something to help me do my work, I'm going to go out, and I'm going to look for it. I'm going to email people. I'm going to go on websites. . . . After that, I'm going to email people. I'm going to call them. I'm going to try to get whatever resources I can get. And so, as a planter, you have to be motivated to learn. You have to be motivated to reach for resources.

With everything that happened over these years and all the different transitions that took place at Valley Praise Church, Aaron learned and matured so much as a leader. We saw his leadership shift from leading a church in a temporary location (a middle school) to a permanent campus (the former Sears Service Center), from a solo approach to a team approach, and from a single site to multisite settings of ministry. Each of these transitions required Pastor Saenz to learn, unlearn, and relearn his methods of leadership in order to lead his church effectively.

5. **Develop trust among the leaders of your church team and lead them to exercise a shared type of leadership as part of the culture of the church.**

No matter how confident and determined you are as a leader, the real test of your leadership is how you are enabling the church in developing a culture in which everyone feels good enough to be trusted with responsibility and to be included in the decision-making process. Aaron helped everybody else jump on board every step of the way, especially during those times of making big moves. Aaron recalls,

> I am aware that I am a strong, decisive, decision-making spirit type of a leader. I need to be like that; but in order for Valley Praise to move forward and grow as a church, I have to learn and lead with trusting my people along the way, because I couldn't [do] all these great things if I didn't build trust.

When we asked Aaron, "When was a time you felt that your core understanding of your leadership was tremendously challenged, and how did you handle the challenge? How did it help you become a better leader?" He answered in this way:

> My wife, Iris, was reading a book that talked about "dying to yourself and who you've been." This line hit me hard and made me realize my leadership and where I have been as a lead pastor of Valley Praise. I started as a solo pastor of a mobile new church plant, and then we went to a permanent facility. By that time, I had to "die" to [my identity as a] mobile church plant pastor, and then I had to be reborn as a pastor who now has a mortgage. And then, I went from being a lead pastor to having staff, which led me to "die" to being the one who had to do everything, then be reborn as the one who learned how to delegate. Now, we are a multisite church, so I have to

"die" as an "addition" type of a leader and [be reborn] as a "multiplying" kind of a leader.

In each of these experiences of "dying to oneself," Aaron is talking about, it doesn't come without pain, hurt, and mourning, as these are all parts of the whole experience of dying. But as we learned from Aaron's testimony of his own "deaths" in different stages of church development, he also experienced the power of resurrection, which helped him become a better fit to lead a growing, healthy, and multiplying church in the Valley.

We hope you enjoyed reading the story of Pastor Aaron Saenz and the journey of the Valley Praise Church. It is also our hope and prayer that God will open up new opportunities for your new church to play its role in partnering with other new and existing congregations in making disciples and transforming communities in the name and in the way of Jesus.

12

When Do We Start?

[Jesus said,] "Very truly, I tell you, the one who believes in me will also do the works that I do and, in fact, will do greater works than these, because I am going to the Father."

—JOHN 14:12

We started this book with these four words: *This is about you!* And we want to conclude this book with the same declaration: This is about you! The only (and best) person who could honestly answer the question, "When do we start?" is none other than you. We hope and pray that your reading of this book encourages you to boldly take the next steps to become an active participant in the church-planting movement wherever you are situated at this point in your life's journey.

As you may recall, we discussed three foundational inquiries, namely: Why Jesus? Why new disciples? And why new churches? We established that your answers to these questions determine what type of new church or faith community you will grow and whom you envision as a leader or potential leader for birthing this new ministry. Moreover, we described who can start new things and how to identify their gifts, strengths, experiences, behaviors, and characteristics as leaders. In this regard, we stressed that the gifts and strengths of the church planter determine the strategies and approaches best used for starting a new church or faith community. To illustrate this point, we highlighted stories of five church planters in a variety of ministry settings, church planting models, and mission contexts. We found that each story exemplified how the combination of gifts and strengths of church planters and the appropriate strategies or methodologies used in church planting will shape the model or type of new church or faith community. We have covered practically every aspect and stage of new church development within this book.

So, we ask, *Are you the one? Are you the one who can lead other people on a discipleship journey? Is it you?* Of course, we want to believe that it is *you* who has been called by God to lead God's people to become agents of God's mission in the world.

As we think about our task of leading a disciple-making movement through forming new disciples in new places, new churches, or new faith communities, we can think of salmon as a way to encourage us to respond positively and to act responsibly to the call of planting new churches. As we all know, salmon are beautiful and fascinating fish. What is so unique and intriguing about this species of fish is its tenacity, courage, and ability to swim upstream not only to survive but, more importantly, to reproduce or multiply. This fish has to take a long journey, face lots of obstacles, and swim against the normal currents so that there will be more salmon in the next season. They are living their destiny, to live and to give life—more life!

Our challenge is this: How do we live this out? What would it look like if we did? Do we have the tenacity and courage to live out our destiny even if it demands that we need to move "upstream" or take the opposite direction against or away from the normal, comfortable, and familiar pattern of Christian faith expressions? What is important and critical to living out our call, mission, and destiny is to begin by remembering who we are and to whom we belong.

In the midst of the many challenges that beset our churches and communities today, and although it can be difficult and dangerous to live out who we are as a people of faith in our current context, we can, nevertheless, choose to be open to the compelling, infiltrating, and initiating grace of God through Christ. As we mentioned in several sections of this book, the example of Jesus makes it clear that living out of our call, mission, and destiny, even in the midst of wild, unpredictable, and dangerous upstream realities in the world, is fundamental to the experience of vital faith. And like the salmon, our faith, by its very nature, is intended to be lived out and bear fruit—much fruit.

Think about, for a moment, what is happening in the world right now. This moment in the history of civilization is a wonderful and amazing time to lead and put into action a vision of a new kind of church that embraces all God's children and lives out its life together as a visible sign of God's presence in the world. We are sure you are eager to be part of this movement of the Spirit of God in spreading God's love for such a time as this. We have an unprecedented opportunity to invite, engage, equip, and release a new batch of disciples of Jesus who will make new disciples in new places and new opportunities for worship, discipleship, community engagement, social transformation, and spiritual formation for many and diverse people in the various types of communities and mission contexts.

Are You READY?

We encourage you to take the next step to move forward in becoming one of the many disciples of Jesus who will make more new disciples, more young disciples, and more diverse disciples of Christ. In this book, we made it clear that our best strategy for fulfilling this mission of inviting God's children to become disciples of Jesus Christ and to participate in the transformative work of the gospel is to develop new and vital faith communities in a variety of shapes and forms, as well as locations and contexts.

As you lead in gathering people in a new faith community and guiding them to deepen their discipleship and participation in the mission of God, we want you to keep in mind some fundamentals in church planting. Living out these principles in leadership will help you even more as you and your new church move toward growth, vitality, and multiplication.

These fundamentals are as follows:

- ☞ The single passion of a church planter is to introduce people to the love of God.
- ☞ A church planter leads from the heart—a heart overflowing with love for God.
- ☞ A church planter is a lover of God; loving God always comes first.

- ⬦ Loving God also means loving others who are dearly loved by God.
- ⬦ These "others" include all God's children—and "all" means ALL!
- ⬦ A church planter is a disciple maker who helps new disciples to become mature followers of Christ.
- ⬦ Making disciples is about seeing people transformed by the love of God, and a church planter needs to experience that transformation for himself or herself.
- ⬦ A church planter serves out of joy and gratitude, not mere obligation or for job security.
- ⬦ A church planter's desire is not to gain glory or prestige for himself or herself but to make a significant impact for the kingdom of God.
- ⬦ A church planter glorifies God in every aspect of his or her life; to give glory to God means pursuing God's purpose with wholehearted devotion.

As you may already know, many more people are finding hope with God, more disciples are standing with people in the margins, and more followers of Christ are advocating for peace and justice in our communities and around the world. As fellow participants in the mission of God, we view our call to ministry as something that is all about seeing lives and communities transformed by the love of God. New and vital communities of faith are effective witnesses when they are rooted in relationships committed to both personal piety and social holiness.

We respond to this great opportunity for mission by asking this question: What does it take to lead a disciple-making movement in today's culture? People like you and many others, whose hearts are filled with gratitude because of God's great love and the passion to share it with others who are also in need of love and care, are needed to make a difference in the lives of people and communities.

Are You SET to Go Forward?

As you take the next steps in church planting, we want to offer the following action steps for your consideration:

🌱 **We need to act now.** Jesus pointed to this step when he told his disciples, "The harvest is plentiful; but the laborers are few" (Luke 10:2). Jesus raised the awareness for urgency among his disciples so that they could start to do something about the concerns and challenges that multitudes of people face each day. As we learned great lessons from our successful planters, we need collaboration with organizational and network leaders as well as leaders and members of communities to bring people together in responding to the needs, challenges, and opportunities for social change in their neighborhoods. Jesus sought the help and involvement of ordinary people to work with him in carrying the mission of God of welcoming and taking in all God's children in the reign of God.

🌱 **We need to build a team.** Jesus showed us how to do this step. In his encounter with Simon and his fellow fishermen, Jesus didn't just find them; he empowered them to catch more than enough to fill their boats. Interestingly, Jesus invited ordinary people to follow him. He spent his entire career with these ordinary folks. He spent a significant amount of time teaching, serving, praying, and living with his friends. Jesus empowered these ordinary people to do extraordinary things while participating in the gospel work of Jesus. Our task as church planters is to look for, invite, and empower our friends and allies to join and get involved in planting new churches. Like Jesus, we should go and find them, know them well, discover their passions, tie those passions to ministry opportunities, work with them, and love them.

🌱 **We need to get the vision right.** It is almost impossible to see God's vision when we are busy and happy with the status quo. If we are comfortable with the way things are, we cannot receive God's vision. One way to see the right vision from God is to get out of God's way. Join God in what God is doing and wants to do in your church and community. This is one step in developing a new faith community that requires adequate time and careful attention on the part of the church planter and the church-planting team. Do not rush this step in the process. It is critical to align every aspect of your church plants with God's vision for your new church. Be intentional in setting aside time for conversations and prayers with your people about the vision of the church.

○ **We need to cast the vision.** Take time to plant and nurture the vision with trusted people from your planting team. When you and your team feel good about it, start sharing your vision with your people until the whole church gets excited about it and owns it. Lack of good communication often leads to confusion and distrust. The most effective leaders know the value of a vision and a guiding team. Jesus taught multitudes of people and kept three in his innermost circle. Do not go on this journey alone. Whatever you do and wherever you go, don't hit the road without your friends and allies.

○ **We need to empower people to action.** The true sign that your church is serious about this mission of making new disciples is when it moves beyond theory to action. As Christians, it is not good enough for us to say, "Jesus, I love you." Jesus expects more from his disciples: "Feed my sheep" (John 21:17). This principle and practice of empowering people in the church to exercise leadership in every aspect of the life and ministry of the church is clearly demonstrated by the stories of the five church planters we included in this book. Each one of them pointed out the fact that it would have been impossible to do what they did and what they are still doing in their church if they had not equipped and empowered the members of their leadership team and members of the church. It takes the whole church to make things happen. As their leader, you need to empower your people to act with their gifts, strengths, and love for God and for all God's people.

○ **We need to gain and sustain momentum.** Make your quick wins known to your people. Celebrate wins. Make sure that small triumphs are visible and speak to what people in your church deeply care about. Incorporate testimonials or giving witness to how God moves in the lives of people and how your church's ministries touch the lives of people in ways that make a huge impact in their lives. People need to know the activities of God through the acts of your church in bringing about the life-changing power of the gospel. Generating positive momentum due to short-term wins makes people excited about what your church is doing, and such a hopeful and happy environment in the local church helps minimize, if not diffuse, cynicism. Every person wants to be part of a winning team. They all get excited when they see progress and how their involvement contributes to bringing real change to people and the community. Never allow urgency to sag. The apostle Paul captured the essence of following and joining in God's mission when (in a reference to Isaiah 64:4) he wrote these words: "What no eye has seen, nor ear heard, nor the human heart conceived, what God has prepared for those who love him" (1 Cor. 2:9). So, for our eyes to see God's vision, we must help one another create wave after wave of change until the vision is a reality. Don't let your momentum slow.

- **We need to keep going and growing.** When your people become more open and helpful in doing God's ministry through your church, ensure that they continue to act in new ways by deepening their behavior in a transformative and multiplying congregational culture. As a community of faith, our work is not to save our church but to serve God by being the hands and feet of Jesus for everyone in the world. The challenge is to learn as you go and to make the necessary changes along the way. In any transition or transformative process, such as starting a new ministry or faith community, you will likely face course corrections. Changes or transitions are always hard work, but they are necessary to grow, mature, and reach new heights in ministry. Jesus got it and rendered his words of encouragement. He said, "For mortals it is impossible, but for God all things are possible" (Matt. 19:26).

- **We need to keep God first.** Jesus produced great things for God. As followers of Jesus, our goal is to trust God and expect great things to be accomplished. Keep God first. Let God bless you and your church as you walk together with God on your journey through transition and the transformative work of making disciples through creating new places for new people. As it says in scripture, "The human mind may devise many plans, but it is the purpose of the LORD that will be established" (Prov. 19:21).

Are You Ready and Set to PLANT?

As avid pool players, we know that reading books, imagining concepts, and analyzing theories of the game do not compare to actually playing the game regularly. There are certain things that pool players need to know, learn, improve, and put into practice if their goal is to win or at least be better pool players. The basics of the game, such as the proper way to hold the cue stick, are easier to learn than, say, knowing the best position to take to make the next shot. It takes a lot of time to learn not only the fundamentals but also the advanced lessons on playing pool. You have to commit yourself to maintaining the fundamentals; improving your understanding and skills of the game; learning from other players, both from beginners and professionals alike; watching the games; and reading books or journals about the game. We've been playing this game for a long time. And, we must say, we are still learning how to play this game the best we can. If there are three words that we have found to be most crucial for every player to keep in mind with regard to this sport, they are these words: *Practice, Practice,* and *Practice!*

Now, if a church planter is a pool player like we are, the next thing the church planter will do after reading this book is to put the learning of both the fundamentals and the advanced lessons in church planting into practice. Here are some action steps you can take as you live out and practice your call to church planting.

1. **Be a Leader.** Effective leadership is required to develop a vital congregation. One of your primary responsibilities as a leader is to lead your church in creating and implementing a comprehensive congregational vitality development process. The primary purpose of your leadership is to find, equip, and deploy your church people to join in God's mission in the world. As a leader, you model vitality through your leadership and live out vitality in your daily life and in everything you do.

    ♭ How have you taken responsibility for it?
    ♭ What is your plan to improve in this area?

2. **Extend Yourself.** You don't lead by yourself. You need to recruit, train, and work with a healthy, forward-moving team who commits to working collaboratively for developing and implementing

a Ministry Action Plan (MAP) for your congregation. Help your people turn their potential into reality. One of the correct measures of your effectiveness as a leader lies in your ability to continually encourage, equip, engage, and bring out the best in others, and also in how you continuously improve. You have to believe in this process and commit yourself to it.

🖉 Whom might God be sending your way?

🖉 Whom are you mentoring or apprenticing?

3. **Notice God's Activities.** Only God's purpose and plan will prevail. Your task is to align and adjust your plan in connection with God's plan. So, the process of vital church development is a process of joining God in what God is doing and wants to do in and through the community of disciples of Jesus Christ. Your leadership in ministry should reach beyond the four walls of your church, but it includes both the immediate and distant mission field where we always find God reaching and drawing the people to God's love.

🖉 How are you engaging your mission field?

🖉 How are you in ministry with the least, the last, the lost?

4. **Engage Your Church to Do a New Thing**. You have the unique opportunity to help your church to reclaim its heritage of being an apostolic and missional movement again in today's context. Be clear that your effort is not about your parish or your ministry but about building God's reign—now and then. Again, the real measure of success will not be in those numbers of small groups, organized prayer circles, or an increasing number of service-project teams. Instead, what matters are the lives touched by the good news of Christ and those who committed themselves to making more disciples of Jesus that will transform the world by creating new places for new people.

🖉 Are you ready to do a new thing?

🖉 What specific tool or resource would help you in this area?

5. **Refresh Yourself.** You are not running a 100-meter dash; you are running a marathon. Things may not always happen exactly

the way you want them to. People will not always agree with you. You should expect some people to disagree with you or to oppose your leadership. Never give up. And focus on your purpose. Therefore, surround yourself and stay connected with people who will point out what is wrong and lift up what is right, and who will always seek what is best for the whole church. Find and establish a relationship with a spiritual director or mentor and a prayer partner. Remember that you are the best person to take care of yourself. Your church's vitality starts with you and in the way you take care of your body, mind, and spirit.

- ⸎ Are you ready to do a new thing?
- ⸎ What specific tool or resource would help you in this area?

We believe you are *Ready* to Lead, *Set* to Go, and equipped to *Plant* a new church. Congratulations! Thank you for reading this book. Please know that you are in our prayers as you begin leading God's people in making more disciples of Jesus Christ and transforming society in the name of Jesus by creating new churches where every child of God is welcome and at home and where the whole community experiences what it means to be in the presence and give witness to the reign of God.

Remember, *this is about you*. So, start your journey with God!

NOTES

Chapter 1: Introduction to Planting

1. *The Works of John Wesley, Vol. 9, The Methodist Societies: History, Nature and Design*, ed. Rupert E. Davies (Nashville, TN: Abingdon Press, 1989), 527.
2. Michael Baughman, ed., *Flipping Church: How Successful Church Planters Are Turning Conventional Wisdom Upside-Down*, (Nashville, TN: Discipleship Resources, 2019), 9.
3. Abby Budiman, "Key Findings about U.S. Immigrants," Pew Research Center, August 20, 2020, https://www.pewresearch.org/fact-tank/2020/08/20/key-findings-about-u-s-immigrants.
4. Junius B. Dotson, *Engaging Your Community: A Guide to Seeing All the People* (Nashville, TN: Discipleship Ministries, 2018), 11.

Chapter 2: Why Plant?

1. Doug Ruffle, "Study Guide on Why Jesus?" Path 1 New Church Starts (Nashville, TN: Discipleship Ministries of The United Methodist Church), used with permission.
2. *John Wesley's Works*, Third Edition, vol. 1. (Kansas City, MO: Beacon Hill Press, reprinted 1986), 103.
3. "A Lewis Center Report on New People Through New Places," Lewis Center for Church Leadership, Wesley Theological Seminary, November 2017, 3–5.

4. Jim Griffith and Bill Easum, *Ten Most Common Mistakes Made by New Church Starts* (St. Louis, MO: Chalice Press, 2008), 6.

Chapter 8: What Is a New Faith Community?

1. Dirk Elliot, *Vital Merger: A New Church Start Approach That Joins Church Families Together* (New Castle, DE: Fun and Done Press, 2013).

Chapter 9: What Leads to Where

1. "How It All Started," The Nett Church, http://www.thenettchurch.com/our-story.

Chapter 10: Where to Plant?

1. "How Much of an Iceberg is Below the Water," Navigation Center, United States Coast Guard, U.S. Department of Homeland Security, https://www.navcen.uscg.gov/?pageName=iipHowMuchOfAnIceberg IsBelowTheWater.
2. John Wesley, Sermon 85, "On Working Out Our Own Salvation," §§4. III.4, in *The Sermons of John Wesley*, ed. Thomas Jackson, Wesley Center Online, http://wesley.nnu.edu/john-wesley/the-sermons-of-john-wesley-1872-edition/sermon-85-on-working-out-our-own-salvation/.
3. Leonardo Boff, *Ecclesiogenesis: The Base Communities Reinvent the Church* (Maryknoll, NY: Orbis, 1986), location 509 Kindle.
4. Dale Carnegie. *How to Win Friends and Influence People* (New York: Simon & Schuster, 1936), 118.